Introduction to

Music Education

by

RUSSEL N. SQUIRE, Ph.D.

PROFESSOR OF MUSIC
GEORGE PEPPERDINE COLLEGE

WITH A FOREWORD AND AN APPENDIX BY
KARL W. GEHRKENS
Professor Emeritus of Music Education, Oberlin College

THE RONALD PRESS COMPANY ⸱ NEW YORK

2

Library of Congress Catalog Card Number: 52–6191

PRINTED IN THE UNITED STATES OF AMERICA

TO MY WIFE

DORIS WINIFRED ORR SQUIRE

FOREWORD

This book grew out of a seminar in music education that Dr. Squire and I conducted at the Roosevelt College School of Music in Chicago. In preparation for this project, Dr. Squire did a great deal of reading and research, and his lectures seemed to me to be so penetrating and illuminating that I suggested to him that he organize and redevelop the material for publication in book form. So he revised and expanded his lectures, and the result is this valuable book.

Most books on music education deal only with trivia—they discuss "methods of teaching," and often there is but little of either philosophy or psychology in them. But Dr. Squire has gone back of even the most psychologically devised methods and procedures to the philosophical and sociological tenets on which the whole fabric of "education through music" is based. For this reason I consider his volume to be an important addition to the still comparatively small amount of literature dealing with the teaching of music to "all the children of all the people."

My own direct contribution to the book has been slight, consisting only of an appendix in which I attempt to differentiate between philosophy and psychology and to pose a number of questions and problems concerning the philosophy and psychology of music teaching in schools. Chapter 3, "Educational Continuity at Different Levels," is also based on a manuscript of mine, this having been done with full approval and permission.

KARL W. GEHRKENS

PREFACE

The purpose of this volume is to provide an orientation in music education that will be useful to the student preparing to teach music, to the general educator responsible for school administration, and to the in-service teacher responsible for all or part of his school's music program. To help the reader gain a broad perspective on music education in this country, considerable emphasis is given throughout the work to philosophical, psychological, and sociological considerations. In addition, a careful examination is made of the functions, curriculum, and methodological principles of music education on the several levels from kindergarten through college.

The volume has been organized to serve as a textbook for college courses that attempt to survey music education as a whole. Six categories of interest are treated: (1) the historical roots of music education in the United States; (2) the place of music in life and in education for democracy; (3) continuity and articulation among the several age groups of pupils; (4) the function of music in the schools for each age group; (5) the problems confronting music education today; and (6) musical aptitude testing. The questions and exercises at the end of each chapter suggest topics for class discussion, and the extensive annotated bibliography should be useful to those who wish to study topics beyond the scope of this work.

Attention is called to the report in Chapter 8 on the numerous curricular plans and degrees in music offered by the colleges and junior colleges in the United States, and to the tables showing the credit allowed by various colleges for private music lessons. This material is the result of a survey which I made, and to the many colleges who responded to my queries I wish to express my thanks.

Because it is important that persons interested in music education bring into focus all the visible configuration of their field, it is hoped that the reader at whatever level of special interest will find himself moved to read the material pertaining to all the other educational levels. The value in such continuity of reading interest is aptly set forth in Chapter 3, which is based upon an unpublished manuscript by Karl W. Gehrkens.

This brings me to the point where I wish to thank Dr. Gehrkens, my present as well as former teacher and benefactor, for encouraging me to prepare this volume, and for performing that most arduous and unrewarding of all tasks —reading the material and giving me invaluable suggestions and assistance. Included at the end of the volume is an appendix by Dr. Gehrkens, generously prepared in order to help fulfill the purpose of the book.

I wish also to thank Dr. Earl V. Pullias, Professor of Psychology and Dean of George Pepperdine College, who has always been generous, kind, and helpful in responding to my frequent calls upon him for advice and aid. I am indebted, too, to Miss Lorene Wells, a competent assistant, who brings to her work those rare attributes, good judgment and good taste. To others who painstakingly read the manuscript and rendered important help, I wish to express my thanks.

RUSSEL N. SQUIRE

Los Angeles
January, 1952

CONTENTS

INTRODUCTION TO
MUSIC EDUCATION

Chapter 1

THE HISTORY OF MUSIC EDUCATION IN THE UNITED STATES

Colonial Days

Conditions during colonial days were not conducive to the development of a rich artistic life, and up to the nineteenth century our country, musically speaking, was decidedly barren. It is reported that in 1673 there were no "musicians by trade" in the New World,[1] and the first instance on record of advertising by a music teacher appeared in a Charleston, South Carolina, newspaper in 1730. Of course church music, and particularly psalmody, were well established in a number of places early in the eighteenth century, and several choral societies came into existence between 1750 and 1800. But such concert life as there was depended almost exclusively on European artists. The idea of including music as a serious study in schools and colleges did not take root until nearly the middle of the nineteenth century and did not actually come to any sort of tangible fruition until the twentieth.

It was the influx of immigrants from Europe, and especially from Germany, that probably gave the greatest impetus to our musical life during the first half of the nineteenth century, and the enormous number of immigrants who made America their permanent home in the forty or fifty years following the Civil War entirely changed

[1] Louis C. Elson, *The History of American Music* (New York: The Macmillan Co., 1925), p. 8. Quotation from *Observations Made by the Curious in New England* (London: 1673).

the complexion of our artistic life. A large majority of our musicians, both performers and teachers, were of foreign birth even as late as 1900, and it is only during the present century that the United States has become independent, musically speaking.

The Singing School

Music education in the United States is rooted in the early singing school, which had its official beginning in 1712 when the Reverend John Tufts of Newberry published a treatise [2] on how to sing. For almost a hundred years before 1712, the condition of singing in the churches of the colonies had been, in general, at a very low ebb. The singing school came into being in order to improve the singing of the members of the church congregations of the day.

In the 1600's there was only the singing of metrical versions of the Psalms by church congregations. By 1750 the hymns of Isaac Watts and Charles Wesley were becoming known, but the singing was still mostly of a crude kind; the teaching of tunes was almost entirely by ear, and there was but little effort to make church music an art. In a few churches, however, those members with the best voices began to sit together, and out of this custom arose the church choir. From the church choir there developed the need for instruction in music reading, which accounts for the rise of the "singing school," and ultimately for many other important musical developments.

Records are meager and incomplete, but it is known that as early as 1721 there was a singing school [3] in Boston; that in 1741 the Moravian Brethren had established schools in

[2] A *Very Plain and Easy Introduction to the Whole Art of Singing Psalm Tunes.*

[3] From diary accounts by Dr. Samuel Sewall. Reports have it that singing schools were in existence in Boston in 1717.

Bethlehem, Pennsylvania; and that by 1750 there were schools not only in the large cities such as Boston, New York, and Philadelphia, but also in many other places. It should be understood that the early singing schools were merely groups of persons who met more or less regularly—usually in the evening—for instruction in choral singing and the rudiments of music. The leader or teacher was a member of the community who liked music, probably had a good natural voice, and had taught himself the elements of music. The *sol-fa* syllables were used as the basis of instruction, and the motivating force—at least at the beginning—was the desire to improve church music.

The singing school carried on throughout the eighteenth century and well on into the nineteenth century. After the Civil War there was a later development of the singing school, known as the "community festival." The Worcester Musical Convention started in 1858 as an outcropping or a last development of the singing school, and by 1876 all characteristics of the earlier singing school were lost. Of course, there are places in the country, even today, where singing schools, in direct connection with church congregational singing activities, are supported.

Some of the early music leaders were Andrew Adgate, Francis Hopkinson, James Lyon, and William Billings. The early singing schools, although they at first dealt exclusively with church music, gradually expanded their musical horizon, and from them are to be traced at least two important developments: (1) the enormous popularity of the oratorio society, especially in New England; and (2) the rise of music teaching in the public schools. The singing school thus has great historical significance, and it is generally considered as the real beginning of music education in America.

Early in the nineteenth century another musical phase began to develop: concerts by artists became more frequent, and the singing-school teacher developed into a much better musician. It was at this time that Lowell Mason (1792–1872) came upon the scene, and although this famous gentleman was a bank clerk for fifteen years before he became a professional musician, he has had, nevertheless, an enormous influence, first, upon church music, through his volume of hymns and choruses entitled *The Handel and Haydn Collection* together with his ensuing connection with music in several Boston churches; and, second, upon education, by his contention that all children are musical, that they all ought to learn to sing, and that music ought therefore to be taught in the public schools as a regular subject of instruction.

It was out of his experience with the singing school that Mason conceived the idea of public school education. Now, at this time, Pestalozzi was having considerable success in teaching children in Switzerland to sing. Mason felt that similar success could be achieved in the United States. And so, without compensation, he demonstrated to the school board of Boston (1837–38) through a year's teaching of singing to children in public schools that music as a subject of instruction in public education was feasible. Thus, Lowell Mason of Boston, in 1838, became the first "music educator" in the world.

PUBLIC SCHOOL MUSIC

An excerpt from the report in 1836 of the Boston Board of Education, granting the request of a group of petitioners for music in public education, is even today of public importance and interest:

What is the great object of our system of popular instruction? Are our schools mere houses of correction, in which animal nature is to be kept in subjection by the law of brute force and the stated drudgery of distasteful tasks? Not so. They have a nobler office. They are valuable mainly as a preparation and a training of the young spirit for usefulness and happiness in coming life. Now, the defect of our present system, admirable as that system is, is this, that it aims to develop the intellectual part of man's nature solely, when, for all the true purposes of life, it is of more importance, a hundredfold, to feel rightly than to think profoundly. Besides, human life must and ought to have its amusements. Through vocal music you set in motion a mighty power which silently, but surely, in the end, will humanize, refine, and elevate a whole community.[4]

In the last sentence of the report is to be found the philosophy of music education that even today underlies the best music education practices. Because of music's humanizing effects upon the masses, one finds that it is public school policy to teach all the children rather than to teach just the especially talented few.

In the early period, singing was quite generally practiced in all the schools, even before it was formally introduced as a curricular subject by board of education authority. Whenever such authority was pronounced and formal introduction of music as a school subject was advised, then in most cases a special music teacher was appointed. Thus, in its earliest days music in the public schools was a "special" subject. Usually the special teacher was not a supervisor— he was an authorized school music teacher. It was not until much later, generally, that music was thrown as a challenge into the lap of the classroom teacher as a subject to teach, under supervision, along with all the other subjects taught in the grade schools.

The appointment of a music teacher in Boston in 1838 was a great event. Later, in Buffalo and New York City, and, as the years went by, in other towns and cities, numer-

[4] Report prepared by the Boston Board of Education in response to a memorial presented by the Academy of Music. The complete text of the report may be found in E. B. Birge, *History of Public School Music in the United States* (Philadelphia: Oliver Ditson Co., 1939), pp. 40–49.

ous "music supervisors" were appointed. By 1900 vocal music was being taught in many cities and villages. However, the teaching of instrumental music, creative writing, and listening lessons had not yet come into existence. After the turn of the century, in spite of the fact that music in many places had become very formal, involving mainly the teaching of sight singing and ear training, an important change came about. For the twentieth century, in the apt words of Ellen Key, was destined to be "the century of the child." In the United States music education came under the influence of such educational reformers as Pestalozzi, Rousseau, Froebel, Tolstoy, and John Dewey. The educational maxim came to be: Study the individual child and provide him with experiences that are planned to suit his needs.

Efforts to fulfill the needs of the child, when applied in music education, brought about an even greater emphasis upon singing. Singing makes for happiness in the singer and provides a delightful and satisfying way in which to give expression to one's feelings. Also, from the new educational view, came emphasis upon folk dancing and rhythmic exercises and games. Then came provision for creativity in music classes. Later, largely through the efforts of Frances E. Clark there came the development of the listening lesson. These all eventuated in the systematic teaching of instrumental playing and the building of bands and orchestras about which more will be said later.

METHODOLOGY IN MUSIC EDUCATION

Another phase of music teaching took place in the period after the Civil War, perhaps from 1865 to 1885, when there were great industrial growth and a considerable emphasis upon efficiency—efficiency in manufacturing, production, and merchandising. It was during this period that the rise of "methodology" is found in music education. At this time there arose the systematizing and the planning by grades of the musical offering in the public schools. School music-teaching became a profession, and the teacher of music was a professional person, whether as a private teacher in a studio or as a public school teacher.

Two important concepts of educational philosophy arose in this period: one, the concept that the pupils should be taught by ear as large a repertoire of songs as possible; the other, that children should themselves learn to read music. And so, the next period, from about 1885 to 1905, was one of consolidating and crystallizing the music-reading methodology. This is the period of the rise of "normal schools" and "summer schools," which taught methods and materials to persons who were to be responsible for music teaching in the following school year. During this period, the *Normal Music Course* appeared under the editorship of Hosea Edson Holt and John Wheeler Tufts; and also the *National Music Course*, which was largely the work of Luther Mason (1828–1896).

Then, after the *Normal Music Course* had been in use for about ten years, there came the *Natural Music Course*. Other series of books were the *Model Music Course*, the *Novello Music Course*, and the *American Music System*. Names of importance in this period were Francis E. Howard, known today for his book *The Child Voice in Singing*; Thaddeus P. Giddings, who made a significant study of the business and pedagogy of reading music; Clarence C. Birchard, the well-known publisher; and Luther Whiting Mason, pupil and distant kin of Lowell Mason. As Lowell is known as the father of music education in the United States, Luther Whiting Mason is recognized as the founder of music education methodology.

At the turn of the century came the introduction, as already indicated, of instrumental music in public school instruction and of the listening lesson, or the "music appreciation" lesson; for the latter we are indebted largely to Frances E. Clark.

INSTRUMENTAL MUSIC INSTRUCTION

Brief consideration will now be given to the function and rise of instrumental music in the public schools. Instrumental work is important because some of the world's greatest music is instrumental, and also because many children prefer playing an instrument to singing. For a child to develop an adequate appreciation of music through listening and performance, he must have experiences with instrumental music as well as with vocal music. Performance should be in ensemble participation, as well as in solo playing.

This emphasis, which in recent decades has developed so astonishingly, is peculiar to the United States. It is a direct result of our demand for and our pride in *education*, without any consideration of the financial or social status of the individual.

The rise of instrumental music since 1900 has undoubtedly given to music in the schools much of the social significance that it enjoys today. In the early days there were a few fairly good orchestras and some bands in a small number of cities and towns of the Middle West. But now, only a little over a generation later, there are hundreds [5] of important orchestras and bands throughout the land which play the world's greatest music with full instrumentation

[5] Perusal of the reports found in the *Music Educators Journal* will show that this is by no means an extravagant figure. Of striking interest is the complete raising of funds by the people of Cleveland to pay the expenses of sending their John Adams High School orchestra to Los Angeles in 1940.

and with an artistry and a virtuosity that are astonishing. Also, there are small instrumental ensembles, piano classes, instrumental classes, and even, occasionally, classes in conducting, orchestration, and theory. Communities are proud of their bands, orchestras, and choirs; and they give loyal support to these musical organizations as they travel hundreds of miles to participate in festivals and competitions. Indeed, their communities often follow them with as much interest as they follow their athletic teams.

Although vocal teachers at first were fearful of the astonishing growth of instrumental activity, they were soon surprised to find that interest in vocal music was being stimulated. Nearly every high school today has boys' and girls' glee clubs and mixed choruses, and quite a number even have *a cappella* choirs. In some high schools there are voice classes and small vocal ensembles. In general, the high school boy or girl of the United States is well provided for if he desires musical training. Many high schools have classes in harmony, counterpoint, orchestration, even composition. In addition there are the usual courses in music history and appreciation. Occasionally one finds a high school that provides private lessons, although, more often, the school permits the granting of credit for work done privately outside of the school with private studio teachers. In general, when private lessons are not offered, class lessons are provided on the instruments and in singing.

Music Conferences

In 1907, as a result of the previous action of Philip C. Hayden in inviting music supervisors in neighboring states to come to Iowa to see his work and discuss it, the Music Supervisors National Conference was organized. This organization has had a great influence upon the development of music teaching in the public schools. Its Research Council has devised courses of study for the grade school and high school, and it has outlined courses of study for training and educating music teachers and supervisors in college. Committees, organized by the Conference, have worked on all conceivable phases of music education. The Conference has set up machinery for sponsoring, conducting, and judging music competitions.

In large sectional and national meetings it has provided artistic and pedagogical encouragement for thousands of music teachers. It has provided at its meetings addresses by well-known educators, and concerts and demonstrations by artists and selected school organizations. In 1921 the Conference, through its Research Council, issued a report which was directly responsible for the first four-year music education training course; this course was instituted in 1922 at Oberlin College. Today colleges and conservatories, quite generally, offer well-planned four-year courses largely in accord with that first outline formulated by the Research Council. The general plan of this course was that about one half the four years' work should be in musicianship and performance, one fourth in education, and one fourth in academic fields other than in music. Karl W. Gehrkens of Oberlin College was mainly responsible for formulating this report.

Accompanying the rise of cooperative interest in "public school music," as evidenced in the Music Supervisors National Conference, an important journalistic service was rendered by Philip C. Hayden, who founded a magazine for music education which he at first called *School Music Monthly*. The name was later changed to *School Music*, and when Hayden died, one of his sons, Van Hayden, continued to publish the magazine with Karl Gehrkens as editor. With the improved organization that resulted when the Music Supervisors National Conference established a permanent office with a salaried executive secretary, Hayden's magazine fell by the wayside. But from 1900, when it was established, until 1934, when it suspended publication, the magazine *School Music* rendered a valuable service to music educators everywhere.

Since 1920 there has been considerable improvement in the standards of music teaching. This is due largely to the development of collegiate teacher-training facilities. In addition to the Music Supervisors National Conference (now called the Music Educators National Conference), the Bureau of Education at Washington, the National Bureau for the Advancement of Music, the National Education Association, and the Music Teachers National Association have all interested themselves, lent support to, and given aid to the movement to give music to "all the children of all the people." It can be said confidently that the people of the United States have become not only music-conscious but music-demanding.

COLLEGE MUSIC

No account of music education would be complete without reference to music in the colleges. In the early college life of America, music had no place; it is only in the last seventy-five years or so that the subject has come to be recognized by the colleges as having any real educational significance. Yale offered no instruction in music until 1854, when Gustav Stoeckel was appointed to the chair of music; Harvard's first courses in music were not offered until the advent of John Knowles Paine in 1862, although there had been an orchestra since 1808 and a singing club as early as 1786; Oberlin College had a choir of sacred music as early as 1835, and in 1837 appointed George N. Allen to provide instruction in music; Ohio Wesleyan offered work in music in 1854; most other colleges made no effort to provide musical instruction until much later.

Since 1880, however, there has been a strong movement in the direction of organizing college departments of music, which in not a few cases have been expanded into schools of music; and today almost all our colleges, including junior colleges and normal schools, offer some kind of accredited music courses.[6]

A considerable number of schools of music or conservatories came into existence after the Civil War. Some of them have come to rank with and even surpass the best European conservatories, so that it is now no longer necessary for Americans to go abroad to study—except for background.

The first college music, consisting usually of choral singing, was aimed primarily at the development of better church music. But with the more general establishment of chairs of music, theoretical courses of various kinds came into existence. In 1893 Edward Dickinson inaugurated a course in music appreciation at Oberlin, and the range of offerings in many colleges now includes harmony, counterpoint, form and analysis, composition, orchestration, music history, musicology, conducting, and physics of musical sound. There is still some difference of opinion as to whether college credit ought to be allowed in applied music (the study of piano, singing, violin, etc.), but the tendency at the present time is in the direction of accrediting any course that involves serious work in any phase of music.[7]

[6] Out of 967 colleges surveyed of the 1,629 colleges and junior colleges established, 942 offer curricular work in music. See Tables on pp. 122 and 123.
[7] Offering credit in applied music toward graduation are 416 colleges out of 541 responding to the author's survey; out of 153 junior colleges responding, 95 offer private instruction for credit. See Table 3 on p. 124.

Most colleges have orchestras, bands, glee clubs, and other ensemble groups, the members of which are, for the most part, thinking of music in avocational rather than vocational terms. In the last quarter-century, training courses for teachers of music in public schools have sprung up everywhere, and many colleges and conservatories now provide special curricula which include the study of both theoretical and applied music, music pedagogy, and certain general subjects outside the field of music.

The Music Education Research Council (at first called the Educational Council) has had a great influence in expanding and regularizing these courses; while the National Association of Schools of Music has had much to do with raising standards of instruction in all phases of music and with regularizing requirements for degrees in all sorts of music schools.

There are two classes of college music students in America: (1) those who elect music just as they would elect courses in English literature or in philosophy—for the sake of general culture; and (2) those who specialize in music with the expectation of becoming performers, teachers, composers, or arrangers. These groups are increasing in number at a rapid rate, and college music is becoming more and more important both as a cultural and as a professional subject.

PHILOSOPHY OF MUSIC EDUCATION

Extending from grade school through college, the growth of musical activities, as seen in the instrumental ensemble, the orchestra, the band, the choral organizations, and the classes in appreciation and history, has engendered in our time a keener awareness of the need for formulating a systematic philosophy of music in education. There has been a moving away from investigations of how best to produce some particular musical achievement by a few, toward the study of how best to utilize music in a general way, as a socializing and developing force for the many. It has been found that merely learning to read music does not necessarily imbue the student with musical love and appreciation. Educators like C. H. Congdon have insisted that the music is what counts; that to be able to sing is what is important; and that analysis and observation toward developing techniques by which one could read new music should come later. William L. Tomlins and Charles H. Farnsworth also have had much to do with developing an interest in the establishment of a more authentic philosophy of music education.

If music teaching in the schools is to be genuinely significant, thoroughly trained musicians must be placed in charge and the pupils must be made to understand that the path to musicianship is hard and long. More and more persons are coming to realize this; therefore music education in public schools—and in many private and parochial schools as well—is being taken very seriously and is already having a very definite influence upon the musical life of our country.

Music education in the United States, particularly in colleges and public schools, is growing at a tremendous rate, and it is through the intelligent and the often sacrificial effort of the music educator, quite as much as from the high quality of artistic performance now so universal, that the United States is becoming genuinely musical.

Questions and Exercises

1. What was the status of music in the United States in the colonial period?
2. What part did the churches play in early United States music?

3. What need did the singing schools fill?
4. How was the attitude toward music of the Boston Board of Education historic?
5. When did emphasis upon "methodology" in public school music teaching begin? How did it happen to arise at this time?
6. What were the distinctive characteristics of some of the music series of the late nineteenth century?
7. How did the growth of music in colleges compare with that in the public schools? Are the aims of college educators similar to those of public school educators?
8. What is meant by the term "philosophy of music education"?
9. Prepare a brief report on the development of music education in Canada and in Great Britain.

Chapter 2

A PHILOSOPHY OF MUSIC EDUCATION

The Place of Music in Education

The business of education is not merely to bring the pupil into contact with past achievements, but rather to help him develop the ideals and traits of character that will enable him to live a useful, generous, socially satisfactory, and, beyond that, happy and contented life. Among educators the question today is not whether *any* activity is a good way in which the child might well spend his time. Their concern is with the question: Is this particular activity the best possible way in which this child might spend his time now, in light of the educative imperatives of our generation?

It may well be asked then if the educational values of music activities in our schools are of such value to those who participate in them as to confirm the view of music educators who assert that they are the most profitable kind of activities in which the children could engage at the moment. Music educators believe that music, in properly administered functional education, can have a beneficent effect upon the physical, mental, and spiritual life of the pupil; that music in education has a high value as a socializing force; and that for those possessed of deep musical interest, music in education can provide significant vocational opportunity.

But more important than vocational consideration, as has already been indicated, education must enable a person to live more richly and more completely, to be a stronger,

18

fitter, better, happier, and more cooperative person, to succeed more fully in the great business of being a human
being. An education that fails to improve the human being
fails to be education at all. An educational subject, however ancient its traditional place in schooling, deserves a
place only as it evidences human usefulness. Music serves
humanity in a profound way and it must be a part of any
education that would set out to serve authentically the
complete needs of men.

Because it is generally believed that music has beneficent
educative effects upon both individuals and groups, one
finds hardly anywhere an educational program in which
music is not included. Its characteristic of satisfying rich
and varied emotional demands would alone give it a large
place in a scheme of education whose ideal is to bring about
the greatest amount of usefulness, contentment, and high
morality on the part of the greatest possible number of
people.

An Aid in Stabilizing Mental Processes. Educators are
much interested in music because it can purge tired nerve
cells of their weariness and restore the individual to a state
of relaxation and poise. It is now recognized by physicians
and scientists that music is a beneficent therapeutic agency
for relieving nervous disorders. There is every reason to
believe that music has important electrical and chemical
and stimulative or sedative effects upon the nerve cells.
Undoubtedly, in the years to come, research already under
way will reveal interesting information about music as a
therapeutic agent.[1] Whatever future findings may disclose

---

[1] The basic idea behind the use of music in therapy is that the response
to music, being a primitive thing, is not mediated through the master brain,
but through the thalamus. The mentally ill person may build up a wall
between himself and verbal and associative reality, but he has no defense
against impulses which go directly to the thalamus, the seat of the emotions, the "switchboard" for sensory stimuli. Therefore the therapist believes

about the details of its function, music is now included in the curriculum of nearly every educational institution of the country because its benefits are so obvious.

An Aid in Developing Intellect. There is an interesting relic of earlier days in educational theory when various subjects of education were viewed as "mind trainers." In the last several years the more progressive educational areas have devoted little attention to this concept. But long ago it was widely believed that a person should study algebra, for example, in order to develop acuteness of thinking, and that the rapidity and the clearness of thinking which he learned in algebra would be "transferable" to other activities of living. In general, educators do not believe very much in the transfer of training from one subject to another except as the factors in one subject are *identical* with the factors in a second subject of study and activity. Perhaps in the older educational traditions, whatever transfer of training there might have been was not as readily gained because too often the subject matter being taught so methodically, as in the case of algebra, for instance, was really not highly useful in everyday living or applicable to many situations of everyday life.

But music is a subject of general use to a great many people much of the time. It is a study of high intrinsic cultural values; and it exerts, as shall be indicated, a definite influence in sharpening the intellect. It is no longer regarded

---

that he can "surprise" the patient through music which gets into the patient's consciousness and arouses in him bits of reality which, as brought up by the music, serve as bridges on which the patient is enabled to build a greater contact with reality. If the psychiatrist or physician can get the patient to listen to music and accept its associations, then the patient may soon be reached again through verbal techniques, after which more advanced psychotherapy can begin. (Dorothy M. Schullian and Max Schoen, *Music and Medicine*, New York: Henry Schuman, Inc., 1948, p. 270. The particular discussion is contributed by Ira M. Altshuler, M.D., Wayne County General Hospital, Eloise, Michigan.)

as a frill, or an extra, or a luxury to be dropped upon the slightest provocation.

Reading music at sight requires a fine coordination of mental powers. The training in the quickness of response involved in sight reading requiring absolutely accurate seeing and hearing, and the training in observing and apprehending a definite formal design involved in musical composition, together with the rigorous educational insistence upon correct pronunciation, enunciation, and declamation required in vocal music are important values. For example, they make music study an important ally in teaching language. All the characteristics of music seem to indicate that it is a subject which is absolutely unique in the school curriculum. Music study offers the child a possibility of working with material of real and high *intrinsic* value, through the apprehending of which invaluable "mental training" is afforded.[2]

An Aid in Socializing Education. In the last few years education has moved more and more toward the goal of "socializing" the individual. Music is a force that draws people together, makes them feel neighborly, stirs them to group feeling, civic pride, and even religious or patriotic fervor as almost nothing else seems able to do. For socialization among human beings is an emotional subject, not merely an intellectual one. Intellectual appeals alone will not be as effective as appeals to a combination of intellectual and emotional interest. Since music is pre-eminently the language of the emotions, it is therefore the logical

---

[2] Time and again, the author has been told by teachers of foreign languages that good music students succeed in highly superior fashion in their language study—in a way that is notable and that calls attention to their being music students. Similar remarks have been made by teachers of mathematics. There is apparently a strong correlation between superior sensitivity and achievement in rhythmic processes and clear apprehension of mathematical proportions.

agent for the type of socializing services to education that all thinking people have agreed are necessary.

An Aid in Worthily Utilizing Time. Besides the time spent in working to earn a living and the time for sleeping, there is a third period that is perhaps the most important one in people's lives: the time devoted to recreation and to eating. Perhaps most of the troubles and most of the problems that continue to haunt humanity occur during this period devoted to *recreation,* or else to idleness. How can we enable a man to spend his spare time in such a way that he will be happier; that he will be better equipped physically, intellectually, and morally; that he will become more useful to his family and his neighborhood and his country? One way is to provide for the pupil, from the beginning, tools and implements, and visions of what one can do which will be pleasurable and at the same time useful. Such a program in education will encourage the pupil to establish and to exercise an interest not only in music but in history, literature, and other fields which he may thus have available for subsequent exploration during his spare hours. For example, the pupil will find that participation in certain kinds of physical training and athletics will be useful in later life.

In fostering music as a useful interest in leisure time, it should not be overlooked that some of the important activities or outlets which can be encouraged and developed are the opportunities for community singing, community orchestra participation, and for engaging in family as well as community ensemble music groups. In addition, an "amateur" performer of good ability has countless opportunities to appear as a soloist in neighborhood community activities.

An Aid in Educating for Democracy. In the United States emphasis is placed upon the interests of the people. Our democracy is a "government of the people, for the people, and by the people." It is intended that the government's functioning be consistent with the view of the majority—but not at the cost of tyrannizing the loyal minority. It is the ideal to have an unselfish and broad-minded sharing of points of view, and an obedience to the laws that are chosen by the majority—laws which are not capricious or tyrannical, but are designed, rather, to provide order, to protect individualities, and to encourage freedom of expression among all the people of whatever kinds of viewpoints.

A democracy provides opportunity for individual and group expression as well as for collective expression of the whole people. It can now be seen how important music is in education for democracy, when the music is of the kind that realizes and extends and gives expression to the human individualities of the people. If it were possible in some way to have democracy cover the earth, music would be one of the great agencies for implementing the bringing of the cultural values of one group to another, and for mingling the distinctive and individualistic cultural values of the several peoples around the globe. The people of any locale, however confined to the borders of their own province, could, through music, be offered, as it were, a lifelong trip around the world. People anywhere, however limited and confined, could learn of the cultures and the *mores*, the ideals, practices, and customs of peoples everywhere. This would have a beneficent effect upon unifying and giving democratic order to individualistic governments that consequently could succeed peaceably together in one world.

Music affords opportunity for significant self- and group expression and the exchange of cultural patterns. In addition, in its cooperative social function, as seen in the relationship between composer, performer, and listener and also in the relationships of person-subordinated-to-group in ensemble performance (such as choral and orchestral activities) music builds among men sincere mutual understanding and regard for one another. The encouragement of generous understanding of others is thus seen to be a third democratic factor of importance which music in education helps to encourage.

The Place of Music in Human Life

It is a general belief that music is dynamic and exciting, that it can unify whole groups of people and heighten their morale. This is seen in the use of music at athletic contests, in its use at community gatherings and in factories, and on occasions of national stress, such as war. Also, it is a common belief that music, like all art, reflects the culture of both its past and its present. It was said recently, "When we have a better world, we shall have better music." However, it could also be said, "When we have better music, we shall have a better world." For music *helps to mold future culture.* As early as 1704, in Scotland, Andrew Fletcher of Saltoun recounted, ". . . if a man were permitted to make all the ballads, he need not care who should make the laws of a nation." [3]

Social and Communicative Nature. Music is a kind of language which has the power to communicate man's inner thoughts, ideas, and attitudes to his fellow-men. Consider the season when much of the world is thinking about the Resurrection. To say that Christ was *crucified* and then

---

[3] In a letter to the Marquis of Montrose, to be found in Fletcher's *Works*, p. 266; also to be found in Burton Stevenson, *Home Book of Quotations* (New York: Dodd, Mead & Co., Inc., 1937), p. 123. This quotation has often been attributed erroneously to Confucius.

Plato said something similar: "Musical innovation is full of danger to the State, for when modes of music change, the laws of the State always change with them." Plato, *The Republic*, Book IV, Section 424 (to be found in Stevenson, p. 1362).

arose from the dead is to tell a story regarded by many people as of great significance. However, that story does not gain its full effect by mere statement. The poetry of the Biblical account produces a much deeper effect; and, even beyond that, music and songs that have to do with the Passion, Crucifixion, and Resurrection, and are part of the rich heritage of our culture, have given many of us an even greater insight into the story of the Messiah. Bach, for example, has provided the opportunity for deepened apprehension of Christ's Passion. Thus, one can say that music stimulates human responses very much like the responses stimulated by everyday language, except that responses to music are oftentimes more enveloping—despite music's transcending abstraction and the fact that it is irreducible into the ordinary, everyday, conceptual language of word symbols.

Abstract Expressiveness. Music utilizes sounds and groups of sounds which ordinarily symbolize nothing, and which, physically, are made up only of air in motion. By considerable dependence upon memory, music presents, piecemeal, a rhythmic succession and combination of sounds which are to be heard and remembered in time rather than seen at once in space. This piecemeal hearing and remembering of sounds gives to interested persons the effect of a well-worked-out artistic design which stimulates people to muscular, glandular, intellectual, and emotional response.

The wordless sound patterns which make up the framework of music can, at the will of the musical artist, be made to stimulate people to a certain desired awareness or to a certain desired physical response, just as the worded sound patterns of conceptual or symbolic language can secure these effects at the will of the literary artist. Music is a kind of language, then, not a conceptual language of concrete word symbolizations, but a nonconceptual language of abstract sound patterns.[4]

It does not matter, so far as this discussion is concerned, whether the music is pure music, existent for its own purpose and not in any way associated with words, or whether the music is connected with a word text such as in a song. If, for instance, the music is a worthy setting for a worthy poem, then the music is the abstract and spiritual extension of the conceptual and spiritual substance found in the poem itself. In such a wedding of the conceptual and the abstract neither part could get along adequately without the other. What would Schubert's *Erlkönig* be if in the setting for the poem the melody were given to a violin and the singer dispensed with? (It is true that such things are done. But those who commit such irregularities perpetrate an injustice not only upon the artistically sensitive but also upon all who might have experienced the work in its authentic form.) Or what would the *Erlkönig* be if it were read without the musical setting? If this were to occur, would not the reader then supply, subjectively, an abstract extension of his own to the word text? Is that not what Schubert did —give a successful abstract extension to the poem in order that lesser mortals might fully exercise themselves in the most extended, though up to then unsurveyed, areas of the very poem itself? If the reader had previously heard Schubert's setting, would he not then subjectively supply that setting even as he heard the poem read unadorned? It is significant that in the classic Grecian culture, poetry and music were, in a sense, synonymous.

---

[4] The term "abstract" is used because certain idiomatic formulas in music, such as a succession of diminished seventh chords which can suggest a state or even induce a state of restlessness, stimulate human responses without a word of suggestion and without basis in any tangible, physical, or symbolic impetus.

Distinctive Potentiality. Although it may be unutterable, undefinable, untranslatable, that which music transmits is very real, perhaps more real than brick and mortar, or even sword and devastation. Now, because music, by aid of the *memory* of tones, functions in time rather than in space, and because it utilizes the abstraction of pure *nonmaterial* design, music has, among all the arts, the distinctive task of supporting man's efforts in the highest realm of nonmaterial apprehension. Thus, music possesses a unique potentiality of giving to man his most extended opportunity for lofty exercise and expression. What earthly things could carry one to higher realms than some one of Palestrina's settings of *Adoramus Te*, Bach's *French Suites*; than Beethoven's *Ninth Symphony*, Wagner's *Tristan und Isolde*; than the more commonly known "Massa Dear" (arranged from Dvorak's *New World Symphony*), Foster's "Gentle Annie," or the immortal "Swing Low, Sweet Chariot"—or countless other examples of the various significant levels of musical expression?

It is in this realm of spiritual apprehension, of esthetic consciousness, that man is free to give, through music, a recapitulation of his subjective experiences, a reflective portrayal of what his environment has meant, and an *unutterable statement of what his inner hopes are.* However, despite man's freedom of expression through music, and even while the untouchable nature of the unique potentiality to be found in music contributes to its being universally appreciated as a known good in culture, it also contributes, because of its mysteriousness, to its being universally distrusted as a practical means of improving culture. Still, the potentiality in music for improving the culture—at least suggesting improvement—must not be lightly regarded and passed over without at least some future experimental investigation.

The Area of Musical Influence. Music is used to accompany work and play, to build morale, and to unify people's efforts in war and peace. It is used to encourage the cooperative direction of men's efforts into one channel for accomplishment of a single purpose. It is used to heighten the effects of dancing and poetry, and to aid in producing emotional relief and catharsis.

Music also provides needed outlets for other important human activities: an outlet for creative expression; an outlet for response to the environment; and an outlet for resolving inward unrest.[5]

Too, music provides unique means by which to accomplish worthy objectives: a means of apprehending beauty; an outlet for evaluating a culture; a means of diagnosing a culture's ills and, consequent to the process of evaluation, a means of suggesting steps for improvement.

Someone who feels that music has touched but a few may ask, "What of the culture, or historical period, or person that has been denied musical experience almost completely and still, at least apparently, has been eminently successful and happy?" The question is hypothetical and it is likely that no such culture or person can be found that is eminently successful and happy, even apparently. The absence of music might be likened to the absence of clear vision, such as is suffered by the nearsighted person who, unaware of his condition, moves through life thinking that he does indeed see clearly. To disregard the musical side of man's activity and behavior is to neglect a continuously present opportunity to learn more fully about important phases of man's being.

---

[5] The distinction is being made here between the more profound effects of emotional catharsis and the sort of resolving of restlessness which is accomplished in music by changing the focus of one's attention; the latter is also important, although less moving than a true catharsis.

An Outlet for Creative Expression. The creativity given outlet through music is of three sorts: (1) The composer's work is the creation of an original and beautiful arrangement in which he expresses himself and his reactions to aspects of his environment and which he offers "with fear and trembling" to the performer and the listener. (2) The performer's function is the sensitive reoffering to the listener of the composer's artistic creation. The more the performer adapts himself to those artistic demands which he perceives are made by the composer, the more subjective does his work become, involving more and more of his own interpretive power, until indeed he, the performer, is transported into the rank of artist just as was the composer. (3) The listener's part is the apprehending of the artistic creation as first offered by the composer and again by the performer; this process establishes a third work of art as created by the listener. As the listener enters by a subjective process into the apprehending of the music presented, and as he experiences the satisfaction that comes from the knowledge that the composition is indeed a worthy work performed worthily, he can be carried into an ecstasy—not into an ecstasy induced by the composer alone or by the performer alone but partly by each and partly by both together, and perhaps mostly by his own subjective power by which, as a listener, he gives his own spiritual extension to the work, just as the composer did when he gave birth and development to the work's inherent spirit in the first place. The listener, if he is artistically sensitive, is empowered in some inexplicable way to keep the work of the composer, even as it is being performed, separate from the work of the performer, so that he can with assurance say that the composition was fine but the rendition was poor, or that the rendition was superb but that it was a pity the composition did not deserve such an admirable performance.

The listener, in greater and greater degree as his apprehension grows and as his subjective self enters into that apprehension, contributes the products of his own stimulated imagination to the artistic offerings presented. Thus the listener is transported into the rank of true artist just as were the composer and the performer. Although the listener's creation may be mostly unavailable to others, it is not entirely so. The stimulation from the music evidences itself in the listener's demeanor, sometimes to such an extent that its contagion affects other listeners who are present, even though they be less sensitive. Indeed, it is not to be overlooked that many of the most sensitive listeners choose to develop themselves in the art of criticism and to become professional *critics*; and to be a critic is to assume a grave responsibility. In a sense, the critic is trying to give translation to the unspeakable. There are indeed few persons passing as critics who can live up to the dignity of their task.

The manifold nature of musical creativity, as indicated above, and which is evidenced in man's processes, is in magnitude and complexity utterly beyond human comprehension or appraisal. Throughout the ages, the effect of music upon man has been overwhelming. This is due to the power of creative expression through music, which is given not merely to a few but to the larger proportion of mankind. Because of the effect of music upon man, the potentiality of musical creativity in the lives of men, for good or for evil, must not be underestimated. Especially should this potentiality be considered when it is remembered that the creativity given life in music affects not only the composer and the performer but every listener too.

The creative outlet which music provides for man, transporting him into a transcending realm where he can speak the unspeakable and give substance to what otherwise would be mere intuitive fantasy, gives to the human being an objective extension of his power of insight and an increase in the number of ways in which he can interpretively communicate his reactions.

Since not only composers, but performers and listeners too, even idle and inattentive listeners, are affected by the creative function of music, it is not too rash a statement to assert that nearly everyone is being moved, for good or for evil, by some kind of music.

An Outlet for Response to the Environment. The art of music provides a medium through which man can reflect his environment and his experiences, or reproduce them ideally. That is, through music man can respond to, or give recapitulation to, his experiences; and, also, if he desires, he can give them a transformed, idealized portrayal in terms of what he longs for or of what he hoped they might have been. The opportunity given man for presenting in artistic works of music a view of his environment and heritage is one of considerable significance. Involving the manifold complications of the creative processes already suggested, the musical response to environment bases itself upon significant insight into, and apprehension of, *eternal beauty*. This musical response to environment affects man in ways that satisfy his demands for organic balance and proportion —demands that are themselves a manifestation of his striving for spiritual beauty or everlasting life. An artistic work of music is the direct product of its environment through the agency of man's creation, and it manifests variation in its substance in direct relation to variation in the environment. The artistic exercising of such response to, or reflection of, environment can include also a *pointing of the way to improvement* of some of the factors in the environment. This is possible because the accumulating of created music as modified by the environment has reciprocally ever-in-creasing weight as it itself becomes part of the environment and modifies the future environment. That music which *ideally* has reproduced reactions to past environmental factors in terms of imagined and longed-for objectives will give helpful impetus to the improvement of future environment.

An Outlet for Resolving Inward Unrest. Through music, man can resolve a persistent striving that arises out of a certain untouchable organic unrest and thus provide for himself satisfying relief. That certain stimuli in the environ-ment can receive satisfactory solution only through music is the case because in the area of the "unutterable" only music can give the power of expression to man. By the agency of conceptual or word-text language the meaning of the other arts and crafts can be communicated, to some small degree at least, from one person to another. But the meaning in music is not to be conveyed through the agency of such language. As has already been indicated, expression and communication of some kinds of intuitions can take place only through music. Yet, although music is intangible and unspeakable, the need for and the importance of such communication and expression are nevertheless felt, and the meaning is readily grasped by the sensitive individual. In this intuitive realm there are satisfaction or dissatisfaction with the environment and a will to retain the status quo or to modify the environment just as there are in the conceptual realm of everyday communication.

An Outlet Through Which Man Can Appreciate Beauty. The artistic process is a creative one by which the individual selects from the environment significant elements which can be "beautifully arranged." A genuine work of art can be born only out of significant and profound insights into the environmental web which not only enmeshes but also supports life. A meaningful arrangement of these environmental factors is a work of art. Often what passes for art is only an imitation of art—that is, the work in question is a copy of some artist's profound arrangement but the imitation itself is not born of artistic travail. A certain deduction about and diagnosis of the state of the culture which has stimulated such imitation are possible. Such imitations can almost always be detected, at least eventually.

Music is the most tenuous and elusive of the arts. It operates in a realm not visible, but audible; in a realm not spatial, but temporal. The art of music must register a sharp perceiving of what is significant in the environment and must not allow itself to be construed as merely utilitarian or representative. Music must be sincere. If it portrays evil it must do so as a physician would report upon evil and illness. Music must not "gloss over"; it must not act as an "opiate" or as a mere "escape" or "compensation" in the bad sense of those terms. Unless what passes for the art of music, or for art of any kind, leads one to the apprehension of *beauty* —that is, a profound insight into positive environmental forces—it cannot be considered to be a work of music or art at all, but only an apparent work of art. Art's reason for being is the fact that it is the road to *beauty*. Beauty is one of the revealings of the Infinite just as are goodness, love, virtue, truth. It matters not whether we can fully identify beauty. The earnest seeking after beauty, like the seeking after truth, is sufficient if we live worthily under the beauty that we do recognize and under the truth that we do know.

A Means of Evaluating a Culture. The philosopher, the musician, the psychologist, and the artist, by examining the music of some long-past generation are enabled to see in that music a definite relationship between it and the culture from which it derived. Often it is very easy to determine from its music what the goals of that generation's culture were—or how far along toward accomplishment of its goals that culture was. There are countless striking instances of these relationships in history. The relationships of a culture and its music, compared with those of another culture and its music, offer an interesting field for study.

Compare—or contrast—the culture of the small religious group that thrived musically in the Middle Ages on Gregorian chant with the culture of the modern day which thrives on the American "gospel hymn." Consider how, out of the institution of Gregorian chant, there arose, with the needed invention of music notation, the transcending Renaissance music and Palestrina, the transforming Reformation music and Bach. Consider, in the light of seventeenth-century background, the eighteenth-century formal music given to Europe by, among others, Bach, Haydn, Handel, and Mozart. Their music literally enveloped the occidental world and helped to usher in the modern era. At least their classic music fitted itself very well into the eighteenth century's evolving of the modern scientific method and systematizing of the intellectual processes, and into the eighteenth century's developing of political and industrial patterns and the systematizing of imperialistic expansion.

Examination and appraisal of the world's history, with any hope of gaining sufficiently useful information for present-day application, are dependent upon study not only of the world's political and economic development, but also of its literary, philosophical, artistic, and musical developments. All these must be considered in making a sociological synthesis of the impact of the world's historical processes.

Is it not significant that the romantic music of the nineteenth century and the *representative* or *program* music of the later nineteenth and early twentieth centuries were contemporary with the increased influence in the occidental world of materialism, pragmatism, and naturalism? Were not the several kinds of music of the period reflective of the several conflicting ideologies evidenced in individualism and socialism; in political democracy and political dictatorship? One might well ask if there are not many similar sociological struggles that have been and still are being reflected in music. Was not the realism of the representative type of music, however specifically imitative like "Music for Machines" or abstractly allusive like the "Rite of Spring," a foreshadowing (perhaps unconscious) of the sociological changes that have been rending the world? Might it not have been possible, if men had been aware of and had an understanding of the prophetic potentiality of music, that a greater number of men would have been enabled to see the vision of a united world, and is it not possible that the revolutionary epoch in which we are now living could have been less rending, less bloody, and therefore less likely to generate unreasoned antagonisms among opposing groups? Someone may assert that such views as these questions seem to outline are hardly tenable. One need not pause here to defend in any specific way the affirmative answers which, after investigation, he might find himself compelled to give to such questions. The questions, the views, suggest themselves when one notes the similarity between the sociological character of a period and the musical character of that period.

Music provides a medium, then, through which man can reflect his environment and his experiences, or reproduce them ideally.[6] Such reflection of or response to environ-

---

[6] By "reproducing ideally" is meant reproducing the factors in the environment that have provoked the artist's creativity, but in the reproducing, omitting the ugly, or untoward, or undesirable factors or aspects seen originally by the artist so that in the reproduction the world has an artist's concept of what can be, or at least should be.

ment, or ideal reproduction of environmental factors, can include a "pointing of the way" to improvement of some of them. That music which has *ideally* reproduced reactions to past environmental factors in terms of longed-for objectives will provide, as it itself becomes part of the environment, helpful impetus toward the improvement of future environment.

It is a happy thing that music, like air, is available almost everywhere for the taking. It is a wonderful thing that music can be a satisfying expression for nearly everyone, even for the person of meager technical attainment who can do almost nothing but listen, perhaps dumfounded, yet nonetheless creatively. Unfortunate is the person who has not tasted of the richness of music and who has, therefore, proceeded through life handicapped, often discontent, torn asunder, unable adequately to cope with or to solve the problems that life presents.

Man longs to exercise himself in the realm of music, and if he is denied that good or fails to use it, its absence or neglect will make itself known as a strangely painful void the possessor of which can at best be but a partial man. To plan the offering or substance of a social economy and omit the arts, especially music, would be to foredoom that imagined social program to failure. That music, in conjunction with related elements of the other arts, can be used to diagnose a culture and indeed to educate that culture is not, then, a hypothesis based upon mere conjecture.

Without attempting to introduce the details of an entirely new subject, it may be noted that ideally, philosophy endeavors to bring one toward the apprehension of reality; religion, toward the laying hold upon goodness or godliness; art, toward the perceiving of beauty; science and learning, toward the organizing and appraising of physical truth. The integration of all these through successful living brings one ever closer to the apprehension of virtue and love. The thought thus arises that truth, beauty, virtue, accuracy, godliness, reality, and love are all manifestations of one and the same thing and that they are interrelated.

The greatest possible achievement in apprehension of all these brings one to the threshold of the good life and denotes the most successful and fruitful accomplishment of mortal man. Religion, philosophy, science and learning, art—none of these may be neglected in the processes of social building.

Without all these there can be no great degree of human integration. Among them it must not be allowed that art be neglected. Dancing, sculpture, craftsmanship, literature, painting, architecture, designing, music—none of these is to be overlooked. For, in part at least, diagnosis of the world's ills and education of its peoples to the better life will involve (1) the appreciation of beauty that comes in significant art experiences; (2) the measuring of how far short of the achievement of beauty the art effort of the world falls; (3) noting whether the alleged art processes are misguided, doing violence to beauty through viciousness or insincerity; and (4) whether the direction toward which the artistic portrayal is pointing is a desirable or an undesirable direction.

Music, in its unique realm of expression, will aid in the wise evaluation of human behavior and, if used skillfully, in the educative processes. Through music the further reaches of the road over which mankind travels toward the ultimate or spiritual achievement, or toward whatever goal man's road, wisely or foolishly, might lead, will be at least partly seen. And thus, by means of his extended and magnified vision of the goals before him which grow out of, among other processes, musical exercise, will man be helped in realigning his course and turning his steps in what seems the wisest direction.

Questions and Exercises

1. What is the purpose of music in education?
2. What purpose should educational subjects satisfy?
3. What are some of the functions of music in education?
4. Discuss one important theory of music therapy.
5. What is meant by "transfer of training"?
6. Show the relationship of music to democracy in education.
7. What does music contribute to human happiness?
8. Discuss the psychology of musical creativity as practiced by the composer, performer, and listener.
9. In what respect is music, of all the arts, unique?
10. What is the relationship of the musician to his environment?
11. What are some sociological potentials of music?
12. Are there any values in "popular" music? Are there any evils?
13. What great ideal for mankind can music serve?
14. Defend music's place in life; in education.
15. Show music's relationship to the people of its historical period.
16. Frame a psychology of music and art in human behavior.

Chapter 3

EDUCATIONAL CONTINUITY
AT DIFFERENT LEVELS *

INTEGRATION

We are hearing a great deal in these days of modern progressive education about integration. The term *integration* means that the several types of correlative activity that under the older philosophy of education would have been allowed to run entirely independently, each in a groove of its own, are now made to criss-cross, to merge, to become unified so that the relationships of the various subjects to one another become evident, and a powerful, unified stream eventuates.

Thus the different phases of music study taken up in the guise of courses labeled by such names as Harmony, Counterpoint, Form, Music History, Piano Playing, and Chorus are merged into one unified stream, the result being a steadily growing and well-organized musicianship of the functional type demanded by modern educational ideals.

Similarly, the relationships between music and the other arts and sciences are made clear by means of projects involving a great variety of subjects and activities so that music is integrated with other life activities in planning a broad and intelligent education.

Finally, all the activities of each individual are correlated and unified, so that his thinking and his feeling, his periods

* This chapter is based almost entirely on an unpublished manuscript by Dr. Karl W. Gehrkens.

of solitude and his various social activities, his work and his play, his moral theories and his practical life habits—all these are so merged and integrated that an individual human being is produced, theoretically at least, who is well adjusted, practical, sane, deeply spiritual, appreciative, and friendly in his attitude, and yet so discriminating in all that he does, that life will be for him a reasonably perfect experience instead of the considerably imperfect one that it actually is for most of us. This is the theory!

ARTICULATION

But in addition to integration there is another principle that is of sufficient educational importance to deserve attention. This is the principle of *articulation*,[1] by which is meant merely what is ordinarily referred to as continuity. It is not enough that we have singing in grade schools, orchestras in high schools, and appreciation courses in colleges. In addition to offering courses in music for each of these levels, we must make certain that the experience provided at each point shall articulate with both the past and the future of the individual student; else we shall have only *period* integration, but not *continuous* integration leading to a unified totality of experience.

The teacher of music in the grade schools must do more than provide interesting and valuable musical experiences,

[1] Articulation can perhaps be best illustrated by a reference to muscular rehabilitation. Temporary inability to move one's wrist is remedied when improvement sets in through a coordination with other muscular movements of the arm. The wrist does not operate by itself. It is influenced in its operation by the operations of all the muscles of the arm. Thus the wrist is moved in terms of articulation—that is, emphasis of attention upon the wrist—but in terms of awareness of the wrist's connection with all the other members of the arm.

To give such attention to junior high school education, for example, as to fail to take effective cognizance of the other educational levels is to fail at the very junior high level itself.

well correlated among themselves and carefully mingled with nonmusical experiences, to assure the perfect integration of educational development in each individual child. While such experiences are good, in fact indispensable, they must be activated also by a knowledge of what type of experience the pupil will have when he goes to junior high school; they must *prepare* him for the demands that will be made upon him in the higher school. Hence the grade-school teacher of music will familiarize himself with junior high school music so that there may be proper articulation between the two.

Continuous Correlation

Similarly, the junior high school teacher must plan experiences for his pupils that are adapted to their changing natures. He must see to it that the various types of musical offerings, such as the general music course, orchestra, band, glee club, and theory class, are well coordinated; and that music as a subject shall be correlated with other subjects taught in this school so as to produce pupils who are well integrated both educationally and personally. In other words, he must make himself familiar with the types of musical experience that these adolescents have had in the grade schools, and he must become intelligently aware of what the senior high school will offer the pupil when he arrives at that level of education. Thus he will build on the knowledge and skill that his pupil has when he arrives at the junior high school; and he will provide additional musical experience that will gradually cause the pupil to develop that riper and broader musicianship expected of a senior high school student. He will also take the trouble to inform his students during their last year in junior high school concerning the musical offerings in the senior high school.

He will help them choose intelligently among the courses offered in the higher school if they ask his advice.

In the senior high school the courses are, at least for the most part, elective. Here are to be found orchestras and bands, glee clubs and *a cappella* choirs, courses in theory and appreciation, many of these rivaling and often surpassing both in extent and in quality similar courses offered in the average conservatory. Both the kind and the quality of the music courses found in different schools vary greatly. The musician outside the public schools will still be able to find plenty of things to scoff at in music as it is taught by school musicians. But the quality of high school music is improving by leaps and bounds, and many a high school orchestra, *a cappella* choir, and string quartet even now outshines all except a few of the very finest of our college organizations.

Here again the principles of *integration* and *articulation* must apply. The different courses in music must be correlated with one another, not isolated from one another, as is so frequently the case. Vocal and instrumental organizations must cooperate instead of attempting, as they so often do, merely to outshine one another in size or glitter. All the music must be allowed to flow with the educational stream as a whole, so that real integration of educational experience may result in the case of each individual pupil.

The teacher of music in the senior high school should be thoroughly familiar with music in the junior high school, whence his pupils came, and with music in college and in community life, whither they will go after graduation. Instead of this, the senior high school teacher frequently scorns the junior high school and its teachings, does not bother to find out what musical experience his pupils have had there and in the grade schools, takes the attitude that nothing really important happens until the senior high school level has been reached. As for college music, usually the high school teacher does not bother his head much about that, does not even find out which music courses taken in high school will be accepted for entrance credit by the colleges to which his students probably will go. There is no articulation either below or above, and high school music might often be compared with an upper arm which has failed to make proper connections with the forearm below and the shoulder above—and then wonders why it cannot seem to function more efficiently. Such an attitude is extremely shortsighted, to say the least, and the high school teacher of music should take a far more aggressive attitude toward preparing his pupils who expect to enter college for the type of music that they will encounter there. He should also familiarize himself with the entrance requirements of many colleges, and in conferring with his pupils regarding a choice of college, he should—other things being equal—naturally favor the college that allows a liberal amount of entrance credit for high school music rather than the one that allows little or none. In addition to this and in support of his contention that high school music is worthy of recognition by the college, he should make certain that his work as a teacher of music is of such a standard that there will be no basis for complaint by the college concerning its quality.

Having seen to it that high school music is worthy of recognition, and having persuaded the college to accept a reasonable amount of it for entrance credit, he should go yet one step further and suggest to the head of the college music department that more adequate provision be made at the college level for high school graduates who have studied music seriously and enthusiastically during their high school days. The musically inclined college freshman is often bitterly disappointed to find that the art apparently has but little standing in the college, that there are few offerings in music, and that credit either is not allowed at all or is given only for theoretical work, whereas he is interested especially in performance.

Music has come to be very important to many high school students, and when they are told upon registering in the college that they must confine themselves to English, mathematics, Latin or Greek, history, and other so-called academic subjects, they rebel—and rightly so. To be sure, they probably soon discover that it is possible to sing in the choir or play in the band, and this experience they accept as a sop; nevertheless, numbers of them would greatly prefer to continue their active study of music and feel that the college ought to consider the time so spent to be worthy of credit toward a B.A. degree just as is the case when they study Latin, French, or history. All this the teacher of high school music must know, and if he adheres to the idea of articulation he will make a real point of establishing a much closer rapport with college music departments.

As for the college musician, how can he establish the principle of articulation in his field? In the first place, he can make himself familiar with secondary school music, take a sympathetic attitude toward it, use his influence in the direction of raising its standards, encourage young musicians of high caliber to go into the school music field as a profession. All this to replace the scornful or, at best, tolerant attitude of the typical college music teacher toward high school music.

In the second place, he can use his influence more aggressively in the direction of inducing his particular college to recognize the greatly improved brand of high school music that now exists in most schools by allowing entrance credit for it, including applied music, the amount to be determined by each individual college, but, in general, to consist of from two to four units. In the third place, he can make a study of the freshmen who come to his institution in order to find out what their attitude is toward electing music as part of a college course and what their musical needs are in both credit and noncredit musical offerings. Finally, having made himself intelligent with regard to the total situation, he can begin to establish a program of musical offerings that will fit the needs of as large a number of individual college students as possible—instead of continuing to offer courses and adhere to policies that were originally hit upon by accident and that have continued to dominate the situation because of custom and tradition.

UNIVERSAL INTERDEPENDENCE

The great lesson of the twentieth century is that everything in the universe is connected with and dependent upon everything else. So, in order to have an efficient life—to say nothing of a happy one—all the parts of the human being— body, mind, spirit—must be coordinated and integrated. In order to have an effective social order and national life, all the human beings in the community and in the entire country must work together for the best interests of all. Finally, in order to have "on earth peace, good will toward men" as a world condition, the nations of the earth as well as the individuals comprising them must renounce their greedy and selfish desires and help one another in a friendly and sympathetic fashion, even as brother stands by brother.

Not all humanity has learned this lesson of continuity, or cooperation, and it is because the nations of the earth have disregarded the ideal of brotherhood that the world is in such a condition of chaos today. But the lesson is important, nevertheless, for the ideal that it teaches is one of those fundamental, far-reaching truths that shine out through all the ages and that in the end are bound to triumph. So if modern civilization is to survive, the lesson of cooperation must of necessity be learned by all. And if music education in America is to fulfill its function of causing art to become "a thing of beauty and a joy forever" in the lives of the millions, instead of confining and limiting its influence to the hundreds or even the thousands, this ideal of cooperation, of continuity—or *articulation*—must come to permeate not only the philosophy and the practice of all music educators but also of the entire musical life in America.

Questions and Exercises

1. In a concise paragraph, what is the educational philosophy of "articulation"?
2. What are the different levels of education that are involved in acquiring efficient articulation?
3. What have been the obstacles hampering the achievement of articulation?
4. In reference to your own educational connections, show how greater articulation can be achieved.
5. Can you show how articulation among "traditional," "progressive," "essentialistic," and democratic philosophies of education might be established?
6. Describe and defend the place of music in an integrated and articulated educational offering.

Chapter 4

MUSIC IN THE ELEMENTARY SCHOOL

PHILOSOPHY

In general, music in the first six grades is a series of experiences so planned that the children's native interest in rhythm and musical tone will be developed into a love of fine music. The goal is that those who have experienced music in the schools will come to find music an increasingly satisfying experience, and that they will gain power to utilize it in increasingly mature fashion throughout the days of their lives. Children's natural affection for music is increasingly developed as they come to understand more clearly the meaning of musical design and structure, musical notation, and music's esthetic quality. Such accomplishment usually comes only if a systematic, consistent plan is carried out through the years of the elementary school period.

Sometimes one finds a teacher in the grade school who imposes such a dosage of technical and theoretical drill, such an emphasis upon learning to read the notes and to "count the time," that the child is glad to be delivered from the musical program at the end of the sixth year, or at the end of the eighth year, or whenever "required music" stops and "elective music" begins. By the time he comes to be a high school graduate such a pupil is "fed up" with music and has found it to be an obnoxious subject which he never intends to explore again.

But occasionally one finds a skillful teacher who loves children and loves music, has sufficient musicianship and taste to select beautiful music to be performed or listened to, and has enough pedagogical preparation, intelligence, and skill to make it possible for him to lead the pupil into musical experiences, delight in which is ever and ever increasingly heightened, so that the child both continues his native interest and develops his power for apprehending and making use of music as a rich part of his daily experience. Such a teacher is laying a foundation in the grade school which, if built upon with consistent vision by subsequent teachers in the junior and senior high schools, will make for a rich life as the child grows into adulthood.

It should be an objective, then, of the grade-school music administration to provide for the pupils authentic opportunity to enjoy and to learn to love a great quantity of beautiful music; and, also, to give the children many happy experiences by means of which they will have opportunity to heighten, fortify, and strengthen their enjoyment of music through increased knowledge about it, increased skill in its performance, increased interest in listening to it, and a more highly developed taste and discrimination in distinguishing between good and bad tone, better and poorer musical composition.[1]

Psychology of Appreciation

The chief objective, then, of music education is what is commonly called "appreciation of music." A mature appreciation of music is gained (1) through singing; (2) through

[1] It should again be emphasized that music has a more important mission than merely to provide for the child an exclusive kind of individual happiness (which should be reason enough for its inclusion in a curriculum). Music and music activity, if they are good, are a socializing agent, a generosity-infusing agent, an important power in democracy.

playing an instrument; (3) through responding appropri-
ately and sensitively to various kinds of rhythmic patterns;
(4) through reading music at sight, that is, performing
music from the printed page; (5) through creating music,
not only the creating that comes in composing, but also the
creating that comes in authentically and interpretively
performing music—at sight, from the printed page, or by
memory; (6) through studying the construction of music
and analyzing its form; (7) through learning about its history and its relationship to man's history in general; and
(8) through studying the psychological and emotional
effects of music on people.

Some of the avenues to appreciation and apprehension of
music are even now open to most public school pupils. In
the experiences that come from singing, the child may be
enabled to develop a considerable acquaintance with and
love for a large repertoire of songs which he will be able to
carry with him long after school days have finished. Too
many times, as has already been indicated, the music teacher
has been exclusively concerned with having the child learn
to "read the notes," forgetting that the beauty of the melody and the delight of singing a suitable text beautifully set
to a satisfying tune are the things that are most important.

By far the greatest number of all the songs that a lower
grade school child encounters are those that have been
taught him by rote, that is, by ear. Thus, by rote learning,
the child will have been enabled to enjoy the esthetic and
spiritual ecstasy of singing as many as possible of the great
store of songs which will continue to be a source of happiness for him. The types of music which a child will have
experienced by the end of his elementary school years will
include songs of our land, songs of patriotism, songs about
other lands and other peoples, songs related to the child's
own experiences in the home and community in which he

lives, songs of the sea, songs of various trades, such as shoe-making and carpentry, virile songs about nature. In men-tioning songs suggesting references to nature, it should be pointed out that not very many youngsters are interested in foolishly sentimental songs about "buttercups" and "daffo-dils" unless both poem and music are written in such a way as to present faithfully a beauty of picturization which is very real, related in significant ways to the experiences that the child actually has as he himself encounters the beauties of nature in his everyday life—and not only as he encounters those beauties in actuality, but also, allowing his imagina-tion complete freedom, as he notices them and marvels at them and re-creates them according to his own ideas and feelings.

In order to insure that the child shall gain greater powers of apprehending music more adequately, grade school ad-ministrators also must provide opportunities that have to do with technical musical proficiency: the ability to under-stand staff notation and key signatures, and the ability even to understand modulation and, to a certain degree, the ele-mentary theory of music; the ability to analyze in a simple way the rhythmic and formal patterns of music and to grasp something of the mysterious communicative power of music as it expresses itself and touches our feelings in the area of what we call the esthetic. Children, after learning songs by rote, will want to learn how they themselves, like the teacher and like other people whom they know, can learn to take a book of songs and sing the songs from the printed page. Consequently, somewhere along the line, perhaps in the third grade, the teacher will provide books which contain the simpler songs that the children already have learned and have come to love. And as they sing those songs again they will begin to observe and note how the songs that they already know so well look upon the printed page. This introduces the use of what is called the *observation song*.

Psychology of Observation and Learning

The observation songs presented to the children are selected from the simpler songs previously learned by rote. It is true that eventually children can learn to sing by ear songs of almost any difficulty. The songs selected for observation purposes, however, must be songs which are very easy and which include only a few of the elements of music notation which the teacher hopes that the child will come to understand. In the use of such easier rote songs, now employed as observation songs, the teacher introduces successively the various problems that are encountered in learning to sing from the printed page. One word of warning: While the songs may not be complex or complicated or difficult, they should always be beautiful, stimulating, and valuable for their own sake, because they have something to contribute to deepening and heightening the happiness and pleasure of the children. And while the teacher is using progressively more complicated rote songs to enlarge the repertoire of the children, and also including certain simpler rote songs, that is, "observation songs," in order to stimulate the children to observe factors and problems and peculiarities of notation as music is recorded on the printed page, he will not neglect giving the children, from other portions of their music book, some very easy songs learned partly by ear and partly by original reading. Such songs are often called *study songs*. It is hoped that, as a consequence of learning rote songs and observing these songs in notation, the child eventually will have had such an experience and assimilation that finally he will, upon looking at an *extremely simple song* (a "study" or "reading" song), be able to "read it right off."

The rote song, the observation song, and then the reading-at-sight song are all important parts of the musical process in the grade schools. Learning most efficiently derives from giving attention, first, to a real experience; second, to observation and analysis of that experience; and, third, to a re-creation, recapitulation, or reproduction of a like experience, although at first of simpler, less complex form. Perhaps this is what is meant by the slogan which has been ascribed to John Dewey: "We learn to do by doing." As has been pointed out by another educator, *we also learn to do by creating*.[2] We have an experience, we observe and analyze the less complicated portions of that experience, and then we learn to create new experiences made up of the factors which we have identified, observed, and analyzed in the previous experiences of rote singing and observation singing, so that eventually we have the ability to read a song that we have not previously heard "right off," out of a book, as we see it for the first time on a page. This is one aspect of what is called "learning to do by creating."

It is important to remember that learning for the average pupil comes from a considerable number of experiences on the same level of complexity in the particular category of problem which is before the learner for observation and analysis. The learner sings many songs that are on the same level of difficulty—fifteen, twenty, twenty-five, or thirty songs—so that he may gain a well-developed experience in all the ramifications of the particular problem which is involved at that level. Thus the learner is enabled to get a full grasp of both the subject and the problem before he moves up another step to a more complex level of learning. And when the pupil does move up another short step, he again stays on that level for some time before he moves up

[2] Karl W. Gehrkens, *Music in the Grade Schools* (Boston: C. C. Birchard & Co., 1934), p. 13.

to the next. It is important that the teacher think of the learning process as being a succession of levels or planes of learning, each successive level or plane being just a little bit —the least little bit—more complex than the previous one. In other words, it is important that the teacher understand that the learning process is not one single, steady climb such as might be envisioned in imagining an inclined plane.

This outline of techniques and educational principles applies not only to the development of the child's singing powers but also, in a general way, to any other kind of learning process. Learning to play an instrument is most effective if carried on in this same way—from experience, to observation and analysis of that experience, to the ability to re-create similar, though simpler, experiences.

The important objective in grade-school music education is to heighten the native enjoyment and to increase the power of the child so that he may continue to enjoy and appreciate music more deeply, and consequently become a more complete person. The reading of music notation and the development of skill in performance should be thought of only as minor or partial goals which function as contributing factors to the larger purpose. Those teachers who think of music reading and skillful performance as ends in themselves often hold their view so tenaciously that their pupils' experiences actually provide very little opportunity for the enjoyment of the beauty of the music.

Ear Training

In trying to develop children's acquaintance with music notation and their ability to read music, there should be a strong emphasis on ear training and tonality training. Indeed, if the *natural* interest of the child in responding to his love for beautiful tone, for tonality, and for pitch and har-

mony is served, a considerable development in ear training
will be the result and an increased skill in reading is likely
to be an automatic by-product.

The ear training should stem largely from the rote- and
observation-song processes. At the time of introducing the
observation song many correlated and connective practices
also can be started. These will enrich the children's experiences as they again sing the songs which they already have
learned by rote but which they now are using for observation purposes. One of the interesting activities which the
children will enjoy is playing on the piano [3] by ear some of
the simple tunes which they have already learned to sing.
As an extension of this enjoyable exercise, the children
might well be encouraged next to play the tunes by ear in
different keys. Thus the children gain a *feeling* for tonali-
ties and learn that they may start at numerous places on the
keyboard and, by a certain choosing of white and black
keys, still play the same identical tune.

Let us take for an example the very simple folk song
"Lightly Row." It is presumed that the children have
learned to sing this song using the words. Having sung the
song with the words and having played it again on the
piano in various "keys," all this having been worked out at
first by rote, the pupils will be interested in seeing how the
song looks on the printed page. Of course, several other
kinds of musical and rhythmic experiences also may be provided. The pupils may be encouraged to march, skip, or
step while they sing the song or hear it played; or to clap to

---

[3] There is a problem here: In many schoolrooms no piano is available.
Perhaps the school authorities may be convinced that there should be, at
least, a piano in the gymnasium or auditorium to which the children could
be taken. It would be better still to have available a small, portable reed
organ. Such an organ may be purchased very reasonably. A set of orchestra
bells will also be found to be very useful in the lower grades.

the rhythm, or to point to the notes of the song on a large chart or else in the book which they hold in their hands. They may well be encouraged also to continue their rhythmic activities while one of their fellow class members plays the tune by ear on the piano. As a consequence of all this, as they look at the notation, they can be led to observe many things—for instance, that solid notes get one pulsation or count, that hollow notes with stems on them get two counts or two steps or two pulsations, and that hollow notes without any stems get four. These items will be not so much things taught or remembered, but *noticed* and *observed* in the normal course of events as the pupils respond to the tune in the various ways which we already have suggested.

At this stage the teacher might well call to the pupils' attention the fact that each particular key on the piano has its specific name, such as E, or A, or G, and so on; and that each degree on the staff, to which the children have pointed as they responded rhythmically to the music of their song, also has a corresponding, specific name, E, or A, or G. The children will readily note that D at a certain point on the keyboard corresponds to D as indicated by a note on the staff—for example, on the treble fourth line. It may then be pointed out that there is another class of names given to these same notes or tones. The names are sometimes known as "syllables," but they ought to be recognized as being Latin names that have come down to us in our present time from their first naming, long ago, by Guido, who lived in the town of Arezzo, in Italy, in the eleventh century. These names are very easy to say and are especially suitable for naming the tones while one sings them. The story of the *Hymn to St. John the Baptist* might be told here, including how each new phrase of the hymn started on a higher degree and that the Latin words or syllables which occurred respectively on the successive first notes of each phrase have come down as the names for the tones of the major and minor modes today—all except the first word, *ut*, which has been replaced with *do* from *Domine*.

After providing the children with this bit of information, it is usually wise to have them sing again the song or songs on which they have been working, in this particular instance "Lightly Row"; but this time to sing the syllable names of the tones—by rote, of course.

By this time the child has learned to sing a particular song by rote; he has learned to "pick it out" on the piano; and he can play it in different places on the piano keyboard, that is, he can transpose it from one key position to another. Also, he has learned something about looking at the staff notation for this particular song and he has, through his experiences, learned to sing it using the Latin syllable names which have such important historical significance and which are so especially suitable for naming the particular tones one is singing.

Children enjoy singing their songs over at a key level lower or higher than before (always taking care to remain within their normal vocal range), and learning where new key levels are found on the piano. Thus they find that key levels and note patterns change correspondingly on the keyboard, in the voice range, and on the staff. Eventually, the children may write on the staff in several different keys the songs that they know, and gain further important experience by singing them from the notation in the various transposed positions. It might now be pointed out that *do* is a tone that has character and personality of its own, *wherever* it may be found on the staff. It will therefore be conceived and remembered in terms of its behavior and function as *heard* rather than in terms of its being, colorlessly, on a certain staff degree because there are some sharps or flats in the "key signature."

The child will thus be enabled to escape the confusion about "movable *do*" which haunts so many teachers and which has caused so many people to feel that the whole business of learning to read music by syllable is, perhaps, out of reach of the average group of children.

It should be emphasized again that reading is an incidental; and where it is carried to an advanced degree, this is done for the purpose of establishing in the child an ear-knowledge and hearing-awareness of tone and tonality. We have always felt that it is unwise, at least in an *early* stage of learning to read, to teach the syllables and the "movable *do*" by use of scales and by reference to key signatures. Such technical implementations may be learned later, when they can be naturally and easily understood. It would be better if the children were to learn to read music incidentally, through the medium of actual and functional listening and producing experiences related to natural interests. Having gone this far in providing syllable feeling and tonality-awareness, the teacher would be wise to introduce many simple songs, perhaps ten or twelve in succession. The children learn to sing them with the words, then pick them out on the piano at different places, and finally perhaps the brighter ones will learn to put upon the staff the notes which represent the particular keys on the piano which they have played.

To have learned the songs by rote, employing the syllable names for the tones instead of the words; and then to put the songs, now in one key, now in another, on the staff; to sing the songs, now in one key, now in another, noting the different locations upon the staff, and how the pitch levels change but the respective behavior of the several tones remains in character—this is an important hearing approach in musical experience.[4]

Here then is what the average child should have learned through the hearing or ear approach in musical experience. The emphasis ought to be upon the threefold process of (1) listening, (2) connecting the listening with rhythm and with playing by ear, and (3) seeing all of this presented visually in staff notation. Consequently, the pupil should have learned to read from the printed page melodic patterns in several key positions on the staff. He may have learned, after hearing a simple melody sung by his fellow-pupils or played upon the piano, to sing the melody with syllables, and then to place the appropriate notes upon the staff in one key or another. (This activity will appeal to the child's interest in learning how and where to indicate the staff location of *do*.) He probably will have learned to sing more nearly in tune, to recognize tonal behavior in the songs he has learned by rote, and to recognize the peculiarities and characteristics of the various tones in the major or minor mode and to sing them with their respective syllable names. All of this is not only *helpful* but actually is also *basic* in the beginnings of ear training. By ear training is meant the increasing of the pupil's natural power to discriminate among tones and pitches and among groupings of these. Such increased power heightens the natural de-

---

[4] Occasionally one hears discussion pro and con in reference to children being *conditioned* into "tonality consciousness," as if that were something bad. Much of the music in existence, even *atonal* music, is dependent for its life upon an apprehension of tonality. A sound apprehension of music's meaning in our time is dependent upon a substantial knowledge of and feeling for "tonality" in order that as musical maturity increases, mature appreciation for atonality also may grow. Contemporary atonality has sprung from the "tonality" that has been so pronounced since the days of Monteverdi. As the philosopher might say, contemporary "atonality" is not atonality at all—it is merely the logical, negative affirmation of tonality.

light that people enjoy when reveling in sounds, and it therefore increases their appreciation.

RHYTHMIC TRAINING

Reference has already been made to the use of rhythmic response in the musical learning experience. Before going into greater detail it might be well to call attention again to the notion of *articulation*. For purposes of illustration three approaches may be chosen: (1) listening, (2) responding muscularly, that is, rhythmically, and (3) *seeing* music exemplified, or portrayed, or illustrated, as in notation. (Such visualizing involves intellectual response.) These three avenues of approach should be articulated and coordinated, else the musical opportunity for the child will be limited. Emphasis upon listening alone (sometimes only to recorded music rather than in connection with an activity such as we have had in mind in our discussion above on ear training) or emphasis upon rhythmic games alone, or emphasis upon music reading to the neglect of the other two (which is so frequently encountered), represents lack of educational articulation.

Rhythmic activities, which children always enjoy, must be abundantly provided. Awareness of this was what prompted Dalcroze to devise his system of *eurhythmics*. Even though lacking any knowledge of eurhythmics as a system, the teacher can yet utilize many important rhythmic devices. Marching, clapping, swaying, running, skipping, walking in large graceful steps, are all gratifying exercises in the playing of rhythmic games.

Many good teachers who recognize that the *rhythmic processes* are musically and psychologically important nevertheless seem to fear that the subject of rhythm belongs in that complex, high-flown area of educational abstraction into which only teachers with magical insight may dare to venture. Luckily, there are many simple devices by which one can help children to develop music appreciation through rhythm, even to quite an advanced degree.

To utilize successfully the rhythmic approaches in teaching, one must of course recognize the peculiar requirements of the different age groups of the children. Children in the lower grades may be given mainly to "keeping time" to the music which they hear or which they sing. Such "keeping time" may consist of marching, dancing, clapping hands, or playing on instruments.

Let us consider children of the ages found for the most part in grades four, five, and six—not only in public school classes, but also in the assemblies or classes of the private teacher who requires all his pupils, in addition to taking private lessons on piano, violin, or other instruments, to meet in groups at regularly appointed times. One should capitalize on the enjoyment that children derive from tapping out with a stick or pencil or clapping with their hands the rhythm of the melodies which they sing. The rhythm of the melody of "America" is a good example. Children enjoy "sounding out" the rhythm while singing the tune, or while listening to others singing it, or even without the melody being sounded at all.

In addition to the *rhythm of the melody* there is another rhythm in which children are interested. This second rhythm is the *rhythm of the pulsation*. This is of course the rhythm indicated in the measure signature. In the song "America" the rhythm is "three-quarter measure," which refers to a kind of pulsation of rhythmic impacts or "beats" which succeed each other in groups of three. Children are asked to note that as these pulsations are sounded, each first count is accented, with the lighter beats falling on two or three. School pupils often enjoy having one group sing and "tap out" the rhythm of the melody, while another group, using some other means of making a different distinctive kind of sound, marks out the rhythm of the pulsation or measure.

There is, in addition, a third rhythm that accompanies the rhythm of the melody. This is the rhythm of the respective pulses of succeeding measures—for example, the *rhythm of the "downbeats."*

In the singing of the tune "America," one is experiencing simultaneously (1) the rhythm of the melody, (2) the rhythm of the pulsation, and also (3) the rhythm of the first counts, or "downbeats" (and also of course the rhythm of the successive second counts and third counts, all of which may be classified as *takt*). Three different kinds of rhythms, then, are experienced at one time in the singing of a tune. It must be added that the *rhythm of the downbeats* is not lost in the *rhythm of the pulsation* as some musicians seem to think. The two rhythms are relatively distinct. It is more obvious, of course, that the rhythm of the melody is quite distinct from the other two rhythms. It is true that experienced adults do not always find themselves as sensitive to this manifold nature of rhythm as they could be. Even people who dance, for instance, will oftentimes be *consciously* sensitive to only one kind of rhythmic pattern. They perhaps enjoy only to a limited degree the interlacing and interweaving of rhythmic patterns. A *conscious* experience of rhythms *analytically perceived* makes for much greater enjoyment in the responses.

It has been the author's experience that students find it exciting to sing a well-known tune like "America" while they themselves sound out, by clapping or stepping, the rhythm of the downbeats. Try this yourself: If you let yourself respond sensitively to each kind of rhythm as you yourself perform it, you may find that a whole new interest in even an old song, which for you has lost much of its vitality, will break forth.

There are many ways in which the three separate rhythmic processes can be used simultaneously, in order to provide for the child the fullest extent of enjoyment of rhythm as a whole. The children as a group can learn to step to the downbeats of a *simple* song as they clap out the rhythm of the pulsations even while they are singing the tune, so that they are actually attending to and creatively expressing in three or more distinct ways the several different rhythms all of which are operating at the same time. (The melody of the round "Row, Row, Row Your Boat" is a good song for this purpose.) If that seems too complicated at first, it is a simple thing to have the children of a class divided into three sections—one group responsible for the singing (the rhythm of the melody is subtly inherent in the singing); another group responsible for tapping out the pulsations; the third group responsible for clapping only the rhythm of the downbeats. (Of course the activities of the various groups should be rotated.)

This suggests an approach for participation in the "rhythm band," which is highly important. After teaching a song in the manner that has been indicated, the teacher might explain that he has arranged some music to be played by the rhythm band (the "toy band" or "rhythm orchestra," whichever name he chooses to use). In this earliest stage, he will pass out the various instruments to the children and explain to them which rhythm pattern each section is to produce with its instruments. The teacher should be careful to have instruments of very similar types and kinds for any one rhythm part. If the piano, the bells, or some other melodic instruments are available, they will be assigned to the sounding of the melody and the pronouncing of the rhythm of the melody. The percussion instruments of light tone quality can be assigned to the rhythm of the pulsations and the larger instruments of greater volume to the rhythm of the downbeat. The children will now know what to do with their instruments and will enjoy playing in the rhythm band the pieces to which they have learned to sensitively "keep rhythm." Some members of the class may be assigned to the singing of the melody while the others take part in the band, and a delightful experience may well result. But the singing must not be allowed to deteriorate into yelling.

An admirable way to teach the reading of music notation in reference to rhythm is by giving the children experience in the three rhythms that always operate when a melody is being performed. (Note that if a counter melody or harmony is added, the rhythmic pattern of the new voice may increase the rhythmic intricacy of the composition.) The pupils having now learned the melody and its rhythmic structure by rote, then having before them for observation the score of the piece which they have learned (either the score for the whole orchestra or else the score for the individual part), some learning in reading rhythmic notation is now almost inevitable. Eventual ability to sense the rhythm indicated by music notation for a new song or piece which the children see for the first time will develop almost automatically.

The main objective, however, in reference to rhythm is not necessarily to teach the children to read music (although it serves well in such a procedure), but rather to provide them with a heightened experience in responding to the interlacings of the rhythmic patterns. In the rhythm of the pulsation, for example, children will find enjoyment and interest in *resting* on certain counts while allowing some other rhythmic voice to *speak* at that point.

In addition to the beauties of a tune or a melodic line and the harmonies that are built beneath a melody to give it added color, interest, and solidarity, children will enjoy rhythmic experiences, systematically presented.

The Listening Lesson

The "listening lesson" usually refers to periods devoted to radio broadcasts or phonograph recordings. Listening of course actually goes on continuously in all musical experiences; children enjoy pitches, harmonies, rhythms, and the simpler musical designs. They enjoy listening discriminately not only to the music produced by others, but to that which they produce themselves. However, it is not at all unusual to find music teachers who have not allowed children time to develop their capability for careful listening.

Children's hours on the radio or television, broadcast by educationally minded advertisers, or by boards of education, are very useful. Phonograph recordings played in the class room, however, allow for greater freedom of lesson planning. Children hearing any of these kinds of presentation are thus enabled to enjoy music that is usually expertly performed.

Music for the listening lesson is chosen to extend the children's acquaintance, and also to serve as a source of pleasure and delight. The more numerous and varied the children's musical experiences have been, the more likely it is that "pure listening" will grow in value as it attaches itself to a multitude of musical references which the pupils remember. But the teacher should be on the alert to guard against the children's becoming fatigued in a kind of listening that requires a complex, sustained concentration.

For the general teacher who feels insecure as a musician, the use of the phonograph for presenting songs to be learned by rote is helpful. Many recordings of the songs to be found in the several music series are available. Thus the inexpert teacher can carry out fairly well a program of teaching music even for developing reading ability. Of course, if the teacher cannot sing, he will not be a very good example for the children. Further, recordings, radio, and television can never really substitute for the live performance of music by a person actually in the room, nor can they allow for as great possibility of spontaneity.

If the teacher remembers that any comments or orientation he makes in introducing a "piece" to be listened to should be pertinent, truthful, brief, and geared to the children's level of interest; and that they should be made before or after the playing—not during the playing—he is quite likely to succeed well in the presenting of "pure listening" lessons. It is helpful both in introducing the music and after its playing to ask questions which will guide the pupils to desired centers for their listening attention. Some teachers like to have the children draw or paint while they listen, thus giving visible expression to their moods. How much of this is wise depends partly on the nature of the music and whether such extra-artistic activity adds to or detracts from the musical work.

The use of recorded music to which the children may respond in rhythm activities is beneficial. To listen to music which the children may plan to "score" for toy orchestra is a most exciting and delightful exercise.

Of course, the children should also be afforded much opportunity to listen quietly to music. But the quiet listening lesson must be most carefully planned and guided in order that it not deteriorate into a passive kind of procedure which becomes tedious or uninteresting—especially if the lesson at any one time is very long.

The whole pure listening lesson of whatever kind, with all comments before and after, should be included within a few minutes.

SPECIAL MUSIC GROUPS

Beginning with the fifth and sixth grades or perhaps as early as the fourth, it is advisable to organize special choral and instrumental groups made up of those who have the ability to do something extra in music beyond what can be included in the normal grade-room situation. Persons in charge of such groups should not be too selective, falling into the error of using only those children who, perhaps because they have had special instruction outside of school, happen to be unusually advanced in the development of their musical ability. It is important to have as many children as possible in both the grade school orchestra and chorus. Limitations on a pupil's participation should be made only on the basis of his inability to perform as well as should ordinarily be expected of any child who has had only such musical experiences as are provided in the normal schoolroom situation. Actually, of course, these groups may be virtually beginning classes in instrumental or choral experience.

Great care should be exercised in selecting the materials for the grade-school chorus, orchestra, or band. The music should be of good quality, related to the normal interests of children at fourth-, fifth-, and sixth-grade age; and it should be of such a degree of difficulty as to be within the ready grasp of the average child.

VOICE CULTURE

The physiology of the voice must be understood in order to make sure that a child's voice is not handicapped or abused in singing. The singing of the grade-school child should be high, soft, and flutelike in its quality. The musical range should be within the treble staff, with the emphasis on avoiding low tones. In this connection it is most unfortunate that some publishing houses present much material that is unworthy of use in a truly educational situation.

Cub Scouts and other social organizations which are so interesting and so important for the child are oftentimes supervised by parents and other adult leaders. These leaders recognize something of the value of music and they therefore include musical experiences in the various activities of their organizations. But they are often uninformed or misinformed about the technical and esthetic requirements of children's group singing. The author has attended meetings at which the parents or other adult leaders have demanded from the children the loudest, most voice-damaging kind of singing. Also, they have called upon the children to choose and sing songs which represent a very low level of educational, social, and musical taste. Such things are unfortunate, and this is one of the reasons why the grade-school teacher must interest himself in the affairs of the community. While it may be that, legally, the teacher's duties are completed when he has done his classwork, yet actually, as a person responsible for the welfare of his society, his duties have only begun at that point. That the teacher ought to interest himself in his church and in his social organizations and community enterprises goes without saying. He should be active, lend his support to them, and he should make those contributions for which he is particularly fitted because of his training, outlook, and perspective.

In conclusion, it should be noted that little has been said about music for the pre-school child of the ages three or four, or about music for the kindergarten. These very small children, of course, will be greatly helped and their lives much enriched by a fine, sensitive, thoughtful offering of musical experiences. But the musical experiences, however systematically planned, should not be the formal kind of instruction that is provided for the children of grade-school ages. Even in the elementary school the music of the first and second grades should be considerably less formal than that of the third and fourth grades and later. The experiences of the pre-school and kindergarten child should be the hearing of delightful music, interesting at that child's level, to which he will respond sometimes by singing, but mostly in rhythmic activities of various sorts. Teaching the child of pre-school age to sing effectively is usually problematical, although he may occasionally sing well the simpler songs he has heard.

In reference again to the elementary schools, however systematic the musical experiences for the upper grades may be, they must always be of the sort that are musical, artistic, and psychologically stimulating; and the process of observing, analyzing, and utilizing those experiences toward more advanced and complicated kinds of learning should be, not intellectually technical, but, rather, emotionally satisfying, so that the pupil is motivated, out of sheer delight and enjoyment, to strive toward greater technical proficiency for the sake of the soul-stirring satisfaction that musical maturity brings on.

Questions and Exercises

1. What are some of the objectives in elementary school music education?
2. What are the steps in developing a child's appreciation of music?
3. After the initial experience, there are two other kinds of experience in the learning process. What are they?
4. What is meant by "learning to do by creating"?

5. Name three kinds of rhythm to be found in any selection of music.
6. What are some precautions to be taken in the child's vocal training?
7. Should the child perform publicly? If so, through what media?
8. Should music lessons be planned? Or should they be produced spontaneously out of the experiences of the moment?
9. Should children learn to read music?
10. Discuss pro and con the question: Should children learn to read music in the elementary school general music program?
11. Carefully outline a three-week schedule of full-day activities involving the integrating of music with other interests in the child's formal learning processes.

Chapter 5

MUSIC IN THE JUNIOR HIGH SCHOOL

One of the educational purposes of the junior high school, distinguishing it from the grade school, is to help develop more systematically the individuality of its boys and girls. Up to junior high school age, little opportunity is provided for specialized activities even if the pupil desires them. But by the time of his enrollment in junior high school the individual child has tastes and abilities of his own which crave distinction and differentiation. Thus the junior high school, providing for the pupil an opportunity to *elect* some of his studies, attempts to partially fulfill the individualistic needs of the junior high school child.

Administrators in the junior high school have been much concerned when they have found that music, which through grade school life has been a joyous and happy experience for the children, has come to be, in junior high, a course oftentimes onerous and difficult, sometimes tedious. Because junior high school music courses have frequently been rather technical and advanced, the great emotional satisfaction derived from the music of the grade school years has in some way been lost. Junior high school (and high school) administrators have been concerned because children who enjoyed music so much upon going into junior high school have, upon leaving it and entering the senior high school, avoided enrolling for music. The administrators may not be well informed as to the details of music education but, sensitive to the desires and attitudes of boys and girls, they have maintained correctly that music should continue to be a joyful experience in junior high school and high school, just as it was in the grade school. The general educator has often thought that there should be less emphasis upon the tedium of analytical study of music. But for some reason the music educators themselves have not always received such an idea kindly. Many of them have felt that they wanted to make music in the later school years a "dignified," a "tough," academic study. Happily the consequent difficult relationship between the junior high administrator and the music teacher has been improved somewhat in recent years. A reconciliation is being brought about, and a condition satisfactory to both sides has been approached.

General Objectives

In addition to understanding the purposes of music education in general, the junior high school music teacher must have clearly in mind the general objectives applicable to junior high school situations. First, it should be the business of the music teacher to provide the children with an esthetic satisfaction at the very time when the lesson is being given. This should be accomplished through participation of the pupils in singing or playing or in listening to musical performance by others, preferably through listening to *live* musical performance rather than to records. Many of the performances might even be given by the students themselves. Of course, opportunities to hear artists perform should always be sought out and planned for as often as possible.

A second concern of the music teacher as he conducts his class should be to prepare his pupils for the future by enabling them to advance in their grasp of the subject of music and in their awareness of its place in their personal and social world. The pupil's creative power must be strengthened so that he may gain immediately, and also through the coming years, an ever-deepening esthetic satisfaction and pleasure from music. It is this part of the music period, devoted to providing tools for the future, in which knowledge about and skill in and practice upon the problems in music are emphasized, in order to prepare the pupil for a more intensified power of apprehension. But it is this part of the lesson which so often neutralizes and destroys the effectiveness of the music experience of the moment— all because the teacher forgets that the child is not so much interested in preparing for what is going to happen some years hence, as he is in a delightful musical experience *now*. It is this problem of the music class which the teacher must solve; namely, to reconcile and strike a balance between musical experience *now* for esthetic satisfaction and musical study now for *future* increased esthetic satisfaction. Failure to solve or properly balance these two phases of the music instruction has usually resulted in a deterioration of the pupil's interest in music to the extent that in junior and senior high school the student is often glad that music is an elective and that he need not be bothered with it.

CURRICULUM

Today the junior high school curriculum usually offers, first, the *general* music class, required of all students; and, second, the *elective* music courses for which children may enroll, perhaps substituting one of these for the general music class. The elective music course provides a heightened refinement of music study. It may be a class in voice, a class in choral participation, such as in a glee club, or a class in instruments, even a band or an orchestra. Sometimes the elective course may be a class in theory and often it is a course in appreciation. Group lessons, more rarely private lessons, are frequently offered in piano and in voice. It has been found that many a child who does not enjoy the general music class gets considerable enjoyment and satisfaction from a special class the members of which are studying singing or trumpet or cello, or what not.

Referring again to the general music classes, it would seem to be wise, although there has been controversy upon this subject, to offer a variety of general courses in music, designed to meet individual and peculiar interests of respective groups, so that any student can find a class in which to enroll and which will offer him satisfaction. Centering the content of the several general music courses around the pupils in this way would make it possible to plan future elective courses in the direction of the pupils' special interests. The subsequent special elective courses in music thus would be more satisfying because of the pupils' previous experience in the general class where they not only had gained knowledge and skill but had also found considerable enjoyment.

SPECIFIC GOALS

There are four specific goals which should be in the minds of every junior high school administrator and teacher. First, the junior high school should provide for the child a "bridge" between the grade school and the high school. Before the junior high school bridge was provided, it was regrettably the case that less than half of those who graduated from eighth grade under the old system survived the first year of high school.

A second goal is to provide opportunity for the adolescent pupil, who is beginning to feel the need for individual expression, to begin, under guidance, to explore and try out his wings, even though his wings are weak and his perspective is not always well founded and his objectives will not often be clear. He will need guidance, but he also must have the opportunity to begin freely to explore and to satisfy his individual interests and curiosity.

The third goal stems out of the second: The junior high school curriculum should provide for individual differences. It must be recognized that each pupil is different from every other pupil, not only physically, but also in interest and ability.

The fourth goal is to make sure that school for the adolescent child will continue to be *life*, that it will still continue to be vital and directly connected with his experiences, his hopes, and his aspirations.

Music, as offered in the junior high school, must fit itself into the framework suggested by these four specific goals.

Thus it becomes clear that the *general* course in junior high school music must satisfy the need for individual exploration. The pupil who perhaps at the moment feels that he cannot spend time for music or does not have talent, or who finds that his interest does not lead him in that direction and asks that he be excused from music, is urged by the wise counselor to go into the general music class for at least a year or two and find out for himself what music is like—find out for sure whether he has a preference or a dislike for what the general course in music has to offer. Later on, after such a period of exploration, the counselor will tell him that if music is not something in which he is going to find great satisfaction, or at least some satisfaction, he will not be required to take any more. Or again, if there is a pupil who wants to take some kind of music but does not know what course to choose, he is given the opportunity to explore, by having suggested to him that he try out for the glee club, or that he elect a beginning instrumental class, or try to learn to play the piano, or perhaps join the band or the beginners' orchestra.

PERSPECTIVES

Above all, the music teacher must recognize that for all of music's importance, it is not a cure-all, or even something that *everybody* must have a lot of. It is a wise music teacher who sees that whereas for many people music is a very normal outlet, there are some children, and some adults too, who will not care for music at all. Therefore the music teacher must again remember that individuals differ from one another. They must not all be thrust into a situation which is distasteful to some of them.

But there is something important in encouraging every child to interest himself in all the experiences that the world has to offer him, and in having him learn to make his choices and to develop his preferences *after a full trial*. When the teacher has accomplished this, he has enabled the pupil to learn something about the scientific method. Thus the general music course in the first two years of junior high school, meeting two or more periods a week, should be a requirement, but the work should be so planned as to satisfy the individual curiosities and desires of all who are enrolled. Also, it should not be overlooked that one of the great values which are especially meaningful at the junior high school level is the power of socialization to be found in music: the developing of the will and the ability to cooperate; meeting the challenge of losing one's self for the good of the whole; working in a music group as one of the team in order to achieve a final goal which can be fully realized only if there is complete coordination and cooperation, and wholehearted support by all the members of the group.

To make the general music class a significant class, rewarding to the pupils and, consequently, to the teacher and to the school as a whole, these things are necessary: first, the teacher must be musically well prepared—a lover of music and children; second, the classroom must be well equipped to present music; third, there must be, in advance, adequate preparation by the teacher for the class period in order to provide variety and to meet the situations that will arise out of the interest and spontaneity of the class; and, fourth, there must be made available to the students several books containing many beautiful unison and part songs.

In order to carry out this general music program successfully, the teacher himself, in addition to being musically well prepared, must be well educated. His musicianship must be practical, not merely academic. He must be a strong, attractive personality. Finally, he should be well acquainted with the psychology of children, especially the psychology of adolescence.

Along with the general music class in junior high school, the effectiveness and function of the junior high school assembly must be recognized. It is there that highly valuable, rich experiences in music can most readily be provided. In the assembly there will be concerts by the school glee clubs and choral organizations and by the orchestra, the band, and the other instrumental groups. Of course there will be much singing by the assembled student body itself. And there will be musical performances by soloists and by groups who come to visit the school from outside places, or from other schools, or from important adult musical organizations in the community.

A second means of developing musical interest and providing satisfying musical experience in the junior high school program, along with the general music class, is the public performance, usually given in the evening, to which parents and members of the community are invited. The public performance stimulates the pupil and provides motivation for his working more efficiently and with greater concentration. This gives him power to develop a greater apprehension of the music in which he is participating; it acquaints the public with the music program which the school is offering, and it is sometimes a means of raising money for the purchase of more music, more instruments, or additional equipment. The standard for public performance should not be a perfectionist one, beyond the reach of the pupils, as is so often the case with the standard of some music teachers, resulting in very few or no public performances. The standard held up as a goal should be the very best, most beautiful, and most musicianly performance that these particular children are capable of presenting.

INDIVIDUALITIES

Coming back again to the subject of individual differences, one must remember that there will be some pupils in the junior high school who are highly talented in music. It would be a tragedy for the teacher to overlook or to neutralize or ignore the high ability of those of his pupils who have such great talent. As has been well said, "The music teacher who tries to get all his pupils to do the same thing, at the same rate, for an equal length of time is a fool." The wise music teacher will be on the alert to discover pupils of unusual musical ability, those who sing or play well, or who have, for example, "absolute pitch." [1] He will be on the

[1] By "absolute pitch" is meant that mysterious ability of some individuals to identify, even under the most trying circumstances, any specific pitches that may be sounded. The ability is all the more mysterious when one remembers that such gifted persons can identify any and all specific pitches

lookout for such boys and girls and will endeavor to gain their confidence. He will probably find that such children normally have considerable curiosity about music as a future vocation. He should keep a certain amount of time free for counseling with them.

Of course the teacher will be kind to the slow pupil, and will give him individual and extra help in order to enrich his life and to develop his skill through apprehending music; and in like manner he will not overlook the responsibility of doing something special for the talented pupil.

In junior high school it is common to talk about the "discipline problem." Bad discipline usually arises out of bad class planning and out of a teacher's inability, unwillingness, or lack of opportunity to take care of the individualities of the various children under his guidance. Behavior is bad when pupils do not like what they are doing. The teacher should learn about the individuality of the pupils. If he knows what it is that the boy or girl thinks he can do, half of the teaching is already accomplished. A junior or a senior high school that provides opportunity for the individual expression of its students very seldom has any severe discipline problems. This brings to mind that in large city situations where the teachers are overloaded and pressed to maintain an almost impossible schedule, inferior educational procedure must assuredly be going on. Indeed, the success that accompanies some of the metropolitan city programs speaks well for the skill of many of the teachers who are working in these large educational citadels. And it speaks well for the planning and effort of the administra-

---

whether in *mean* temperament or *equal* temperament, whether in a range with A at 440 or in another having A at 435, etc.

The author has long desired to refer to such highly developed ability as "absolute tonal memory" rather than "absolute pitch." But the newer term is not usually clearly understood and so the earlier one, "absolute pitch," is used here.

tors. But even so, in a large school on a regular schedule, the teacher should be kept to a small enough load so that he will have time to give ample attention to the individual children under his guidance. Sufficient time ought to be provided so that the teachers may even go into some of the homes and visit the parents of the children who are enrolled in their courses. It is an aim to have school pupils grow into fine citizens, persons who will be desirous of serving their fellow-men. This aim is best accomplished when teachers manifest just such a concern for their pupils.

Questions and Exercises

1. How do the aims of the elementary school differ from those of the junior high school?
2. How have music teachers sometimes failed in the junior high school?
3. What are some of the benefits of junior high school education through music?
4. Should music be required of everyone in junior high school?
5. Why should music be required of anyone in the junior high school?
6. Does modern educational philosophy still hold that the place in education of the junior high school is valid?
7. What are the qualifications for a good junior high school music teacher?
8. What is the psychological and physiological condition of the junior high school pupil? How does this affect the curricular offering in music?
9. Is opportunity for individual "self-expression" a good thing?
10. Outline a curriculum for junior high school music.
11. Indicate extracurricular musical activities that would satisfy social needs of junior high school children.
12. Prepare an analytical report on the vocal problems of the adolescent child, indicating wise psychological and musical solutions.

Chapter 6

MUSIC IN THE SENIOR HIGH SCHOOL

FUNCTIONAL PHILOSOPHY

For the student in senior high school, music can be of immediate and direct benefit. By taking part in music activity and developing skill in musical performance the individual is lifted to a higher level of satisfaction than is provided by much of life. Through music, the sum total of the student's happiness is increased. It is the mark of today's education that, for the most part, the ingredients of its curriculum are made up of things that are useful or that provide satisfaction and happiness, and that therefore seem to have reason for their being. Music is one of these ingredients, and so music activity and music study are supported in progressive schools everywhere.

Many things deserve to be worked at because they are useful and sensible. Many school activities are interesting and even fascinating, so much so that at least some pupils would rather participate in these work activities than to do anything else. The author believes that the philosophy of progressive education is a good philosophy, and that only those things which are useful, provide uplift to the human soul, serve the needs of mankind, and seem sensible in themselves are valid as ingredients in the modern school curriculum.

Admittedly certain self-styled "progressive educators" have at times not been progressive at all. In their effort to see to it that the ingredients of their educational offering are palatable, interesting, and conducive to self-expression, these teachers have forgotten that to deserve inclusion, school offerings must be helpful, useful, sensible—as well as uplifting and stimulating—reaching forward to the achievement of ideals. It is true that the really progressive school finds that the great motives for learning lie in activity and interest; yet a word of warning is necessary. If a school feels that it is fostering the interest and activity of the pupil when it is only providing for him those things that he may happen to want, even when they are senseless and useless, it is not a progressive school at all. Further, because the child lacks perspective and, mysteriously, recognizes this, he naturally asks for guidance from friendly teachers in whom he is naïvely willing to place his confidence. Thus, some things that are not useful or valuable can, in the name of education, be palmed off on unsuspecting pupils. But there is not so much of this now as there used to be, for the adolescent himself is not usually intemperate in his desires and is wise enough to demand something more than just a satisfaction of his superficial wants.

Closely connected with today's philosophy of ideal education are the whole philosophy and purpose of democracy itself. It is not surprising to find that in the truly progressive school the emphasis is upon what the pupil does and what he can learn to do rather than upon what the teacher does. In the progressive school the ideal is that the pupil initiate many of the activities. But if the teacher sees that too few significant wants and needs are being satisfied by the pupil's initiative, he manipulates and arranges situations so that the pupil will come to see, as his attention is called to them, the new needs about which he should be busying himself. All this is because pupils learn more readily in those processes in which they find themselves directly interested of their own volition—and also because the things in which all people, whether young or old, are interested usually are, mysteriously enough, the things that are important.

Of course, longer perspective and greater experience will oftentimes eventuate in a fuller vision, and it is natural, as has already been indicated, for young people to accept the guidance of an older person who, from his experience, points out those things that are important. But if the older person fails to emphasize them in terms of the child's awareness, needs, and interests, he will usually fail to get a ready response.

Today's new education is often accused of being mostly play; it is said that no work, no discipline, no strict atten· tion to a duty are ever supposed to be encountered in a "progressive school." In the author's opinion this accusation is not deserved by progressive education. Play, properly planned, is important and profitable. As others have pointed out, confusion arises because what is work at one moment may be play at another.[1] For example, a music class may find itself interested in performing an entirely new song which has come to the attention of some members of the class. And so, upon request, the whole class sings the song, and, for the moment, this is play. But the teacher, noticing that there are slight inaccuracies here and there and that the class has failed to realize its full beauty, has the pupils work on the song until they learn it. Now, this latter part of the procedure is useful and valid; and it will seem reasonable and sensible to the children who have already indicated that they would like to learn this particular song. Later on, perhaps after a week or so, when the children say, "Let us sing the song that we learned," and they do so, musically and beautifully and correctly, this is again play.

[1] Peter W. Dykema and Karl W. Gehrkens, *The Teaching and Administration of High School Music* (Boston: C. C. Birchard & Co., 1941), p. xx.

This is the genius of the progressive ideal in education. The progressive school is a happy place because it gives opportunity for expression to all its members. It is a place where democracy is encouraged sincerely and wholeheartedly. It is a place where original expression and creativity are encouraged.

Thus, music is seen to have an important place in a progressive curriculum because it provides for creativity and happiness, for acquaintance with the peoples of the world and with beauty; and it encourages physical expression as the pupil responds rhythmically during folk dancing or in eurhythmics. Music provides an opportunity for the child to learn to play the game as if he were on a team, because he understands that the chorus, or whatever organization, will not be successful unless each person subordinates his own desires for the sake of the entire group. In such a situation the child will experience keen delight when, in subordinating himself, he finds that the musical experience that derives from the large group is one of deep and abiding satisfaction. What stronger reasons could be given than these for including music in the modern progressive high school curriculum?

Indeed, in any educational curriculum, not just in that of the senior high school, the musical ingredients should be so delightful, so rich and stimulating, that the persons who experience the musical offerings will want to continue them through later life, making use of music as a source of continued and continuing satisfaction, and as a means of release from the tension and from the dullness, frustration, and pain that often characterize adult life because of the emergencies and the exigencies of making a living in this highly complex and competitive world of today.

Since music exalts the human spirit, high school students —who will soon become adults—will develop an ever more friendly attitude toward their fellow-men. All these releases and satisfactions are very necessary if people are to live a normal, happy life. And the world greatly needs happy, fruitful lives today. In the midst of trouble and tension, hardly anything is more satisfying than the contemplation of beauty and truth and ideals. And what a wonderful satisfaction and release music can be! In music one can be active, creative, and expressive. When one plays the piano, or whistles or sings, or plays the violin, one's lowness of spirit is often transformed into a spirit of happiness.

How glorious it is to join with neighbors in developing a small ensemble in order to play together; how enjoyable the social occasions that can be provided among friends and neighbors in their homes after an evening's musical; how fine to have learned enough about music to enjoy a concert, and to share the experiences afterward and to talk intelligently about what was heard! Because of such experiences, pain, sorrow, and disillusionment often fly away. Only the joy of being alive is left. And during such moments one is sometimes transported to a different world, a world of ecstasy. This is important. In fact, it is one of the most important functions of music in life—"to provide nurture for the spirit of man which the ravages of the machine age are inexorably starving." [2]

Thus the ideal is not merely to advocate a curriculum of music, but rather an *education through music*, such as was suggested by Charles Hubert Farnsworth in his prophetic book of that title.

EDUCATIONAL APPLICATIONS

Music is such an important subject, and has so large a contribution to make to democratic citizenship, that it should be for the many. If it is economically feasible, music

[2] *Ibid.*, p. xxiv.

that will be challenging to the specially proficient students of high talent should also be provided; but under no circumstances should music for the general student of lesser talent be neglected.

In the author's opinion a course in music, designed to serve the needs of students in general, should be required. The general antipathy toward required subjects is not because of the requirement, but because of poor teaching on the part of instructors. Music participation has increased everywhere because of the normal interest of students in the benefits which it provides. A school administration has hardly met its responsibilities if it fails to provide adequate music instruction for those who have not yet awakened to the values which music can have for them.

As a general requirement, every student in the high school deserves to have a period provided in which he may listen quietly to significant music, and in which, as an individual in a large group, he may join in community singing (both in unison and in parts) in a well-planned and well-conducted assembly directed by a capable, socially minded, friendly musician.

Some would ask: Should music be a specialized subject taught in high school or should it be a subject integrated into the general experience of high school life? Should it be part of a general course which includes English, history, art, foreign language, and other subjects? Of course integration with all the aspects of life is always valuable, but one must not forget that there is danger of including and involving so large an amount of material in an integrated program that only slight attention can be paid to any one part of the program. In more recent years there has been an attempt to integrate experiences of like category, such as music, art, and other phases connected with interest in art, into a single course.

Or again, the question: Should the emphasis in high school music teaching be upon enjoyment, apprehension, and appreciation, or upon the gaining of technical power and development of performance skill? Both phases, of course, should be emphasized. It is through performance and participation that the deepest kind of appreciation is developed. Participation in courses on "appreciation" and "listening" can be more effectively and wisely carried on *after* a not too advanced, not too highly specialized kind of activity in performance.

In line with recognition today of the importance of music performance in the curriculum, it is no longer felt that activities in music are to be subsidized by the parents and paid for by private means. Those who sincerely believe in music as a democratic force for increased good citizenship must regard the presentation of music and the provision of equipment for its presentation as obligations to be supported by general taxation.

The modern educator is becoming more and more aware that the effectiveness of music instruction should be measured in terms of the resultant personal or social behavior of those who have studied it, rather than in terms of their knowledge about music and their proficiency in performance. Experience and training in art should be translated into better living. Experience in any of the arts will arouse a heightened and controlled emotional state which will tend to produce in the students of art a refinement of feeling in the control of self which is superior to that displayed by those who have not had such contact. The school should have a right to expect a higher degree of happiness, greater sanity, deeper sympathy, and more intelligent understanding in the case of students of music and the other arts than is expected from students who have not had this training.

Still more questions come to mind: In the high school, should all the music courses offered carry credit or should there be included certain musical activities for which credit is not given? What should be the relationship of the music teacher to music activities that are not in his charge, such as those that occur in the school assembly, in physical education classes, or elsewhere? And what should be the relation of the high school teacher to music in the community which is not connected with his school enterprises at all? It would seem that in solving such problems, the emphasis should be on establishing friendly relationships. The music teacher ought to accept as an obligation active participation in community events as one of the duties resting upon him as a servant of the community. He will of course exercise his citizenship in those areas in which he is most talented and best prepared. Fortunately, at least a few communities have found it possible to pay something extra, beyond the public school stipend, to a teacher who renders unusual service to community welfare.

It would seem that any musical activity worth including and financing in the school's program should carry credit. Of course this is not to imply that more than a certain amount of credit toward graduation should be allowed; many students continue music activities for which they have already received as much credit as can be allowed. A system of awards like that found in many physical education departments is a very effective encouragement to such students.

There is at this point another kind of complication, arising when the high school student renders services, with or without pay, which "professional" musicians might normally expect to render. The conflict between the National Music Camp at Interlochen and the musicians of the

American Federation of Labor is a striking instance. Music educators should give such problems close attention.

Finally, there is always the problem of selecting teaching personnel. Should a school music teacher be selected on the basis of his performance ability or of his social competence and his ability as a leader? If the author had to make the choice between the better musician who did not know how to teach well and the lesser musician who was a skillful teacher, he would probably choose the latter. But today this need not be a problem, for it is usually possible to find men and women who are musically well trained and who have also made thorough preparation for teaching. The skillful teacher who can demonstrate that he is both a good musician and an adequate performer is the ideal person for the school music-teaching job.

There is a problem that has arisen as to the place of music activities in the high school in light of the great emphasis upon intellectual attainment in the present-day secondary school. It is being more and more recognized that increasing emphasis must be given to establishing emotional stability and fine attitudes. This is where music again can play an important part. If carefully selected and properly presented, music is peculiarly stimulating in its power to arouse desirable emotional reactions. Music may thus become an effective force for guiding high school pupils into proper attitudes, actions, and thoughts.

THE APPRECIATION LESSON

Before a listing of the music activities and organizations and the courses in music that are frequently found in a senior high school offering is presented, it will be desirable to consider what is usually called "the appreciation lesson."

As was mentioned a moment ago, fondness for or an appreciation of music comes as a result of some kind of activity in music performance, after which a more academic approach to the study of music for development of deeper appreciation is valuable. But the only contact that many senior high school students have with music is through the general course in music appreciation.

The appreciation lesson provides opportunities for pupils to develop their interest in music—to the end that their responsiveness to beauty may be increased. It sometimes serves as a repertoire or listening lesson. Also, for more experienced students, it may be an ear-training or even a theory and form-analysis lesson.

The teacher's problem is to relate the appreciation lesson to the interest of the pupils without compromising musical quality and thus jeopardizing the students' progress toward a sharpened sensitivity to beauty. It must be remembered that the business of music is to provide opportunities for responding to beauty. Thus the sensitive music teacher opposes the offering of inartistic or bad music for educational consumption. He knows that there is little enough time in which to acquaint students with the abiding artistic values; and he begrudges every moment wasted with inferior music which prevents advances that at best will be inadequate enough.

It is not difficult for a good teacher to choose music of interest to the pupils. There are very clear criteria of good music that will enable the teacher of mature taste to be confident about his selection of material. Good music is well wrought; it shows good evidences of skilled craftsmanship; it is "grammatically" correct in its construction. Good music is possessed of a significant message; it is memorable, making a deep impression on those who hear it; it is consistent in its composition, orderly, unified, impressive, however delicate its mood. In a word, good music is beautiful.[3]

There are many means of accomplishing the purposes of the appreciation lesson:

1. The students themselves may perform music suitable to their abilities. This affords a powerful means of gaining a significant acquaintance with music. Community singing for even the more or less uninitiated has great value and is to be encouraged.

2. Attendance at artist concerts is important in the development of appreciation. Discussion afterward of the whole adventure of attending a concert is always of socially dynamic interest. Musical delight is heightened by such experiences.

3. Listening to good phonograph recordings is a usual means of carrying on the work of appreciation. However, because recordings lack the vitality of original performances they must be employed with care, and they should be used only for short periods of time. The teacher in charge should not talk during the playing of the records, and the orientation and preparation of the class for the hearing of recordings should not be too abstractly academic. If the teacher finds that the pupils become restless during the playing of records, he should plan to use them for shorter periods and should choose more suitable music for future lessons.

4. Radio and television broadcasts are very useful. Television, providing as it does the opportunity to see the performers, is especially promising. The tonal fidelity of television, if the receiver is good, is greater than that of radio broadcasting.

---

[3] Any apparent ugliness that may be found in good music is present for the purpose of making clear the delineation between *ugliness* and *beauty*; *good* and *evil*.

5. Audio-visual equipment making possible class-operated projection of sound pictures is an excellent device for the music appreciation lesson.

EVALUATING THE APPRECIATION LESSON

Measuring the success of the appreciation lesson is an important but precarious part of the teaching procedure. Some teachers measure success by the number of compositions that the students recognize when they hear phonograph recordings. Others have their pupils note on their paper, while listening, the several themes that they hear. Usually the pupils write "A" for the first theme, "B" for the second, and so on. If they hear repetitions of a theme the students mark a counter beside the letter, thus, A″, B′, etc. More advanced pupils will be able to indicate and identify modulations and formal design as they hear the music. Needless to say, the pupil who listens to music with a degree of concentration that will enable him to outline the musical designs on paper will usually be able to recognize the compositions in the future. This kind of measuring has some ear-training values. Unfortunately, it is doubtful if arbitrary insistence upon such measuring procedures will assure an increase in the pupils' love for music or their sensitivity to beauty. The teacher should watch constantly and carefully to see whether the devices he is using are being met with interest on the part of the pupils. In general, it is better to use devices that are directly functional in their relation to the students' interest than those that seem to be artificial.

It would seem that noting how the pupils' faces light up when they hear good music, how often they ask for certain compositions that have been heard before, with what insight they voluntarily criticize selections of music, and, finally, whether the students evidence initiative in selecting music and attending concerts, would be the best ways to measure the success of the appreciation lessons.

Using recognition lists or, in the case of very experienced music pupils, having the students work out analyses while listening, are valuable teaching procedures; and no doubt the pupils themselves will enthusiastically accept such methods as good practice and drill by which they can measure for themselves their increasing listening ability. However, such techniques should be used rarely, if ever, to measure their love for music.

CURRICULAR OFFERING

In large metropolitan senior high schools numerous music courses and activities are offered. Much is being done also to provide for the individualities of the multitudes of senior high school students.

It was found in a study [4] carried on during 1931–32 that of 139 "gifted children" in elementary school, 14 per cent were highly talented in music. Of this 14 per cent, the median I.Q. was 121 in a range from 95 to 154. Of the junior high school group, 25 per cent of the highly gifted were highly talented in music. They ranged in I.Q. from 90 to 154, the median being 118. A large percentage of all the gifted children were found to be superior in mental, moral, and physical traits and abilities. The greater number were found to possess a "pleasing personality." Over 92 per cent were credited with "all around development." A few were found to need help in adjustment to life. These were serviced by the Behavior Research Clinic.

In carrying on the continuing study of gifted children of

[4] A Report of a Study of Gifted Children by the Public Schools of Berkeley, California, August, 1937.

all kinds of interest, the report states that allowing individual students to present musical solos and enabling pupils to perform in music organizations are beneficial to all students, but of course mostly to those who are gifted in music. It would seem that much might be accomplished in musical areas that could well point the way to what might be done in many other areas of educational activity.

There is also an important opportunity to serve the needs of retarded children through music. Strockbine reports [5] that in his work with dull children he finds frequently they have musical abilities favorably comparable with those of more normal privilege. Contrary to popular opinion, he says, the dull children have traits of individuality just like normal and gifted children; and music serves their needs just as it does those of the other children.

The following listing is a fair representation of the offerings in numerous senior high schools:

I. Activities

   Assembly Singing
   Boys' Glee Clubs (One to three clubs of different degrees of advancement)
   Girls' Glee Clubs (One to three clubs of different degrees of advancement)
   Mixed Choruses (Sometimes as many as three organizations of different degrees of advancement)
   Special Choruses (A *cappella* or operatic)
   Voice Classes (Often several of these, sometimes operated and organized like the choruses)
   Instrumental Classes (Band instruments, orchestra instruments, and piano)
   Beginning Band (Sometimes organized as substitute for instrumental classes)
   Intermediate Band

[5] Frank Strockbine, Jr. "Music for Retarded Children," *Educational Music Magazine*, January, 1951.

Advanced Band (Concert band and marching band)
Beginning Orchestra
Intermediate Orchestra
Advanced Orchestra (Often of full symphonic proportions)
Special Instrumental Ensembles (String quartets, woodwind
quintets, etc.)

II. Courses offered in "major" and "minor" sequences leading to graduation

Musicianship
Beginning Harmony
Intermediate Harmony
Advanced Harmony
Beginning Orchestration
Beginning History and Appreciation of Music
Advanced History and Appreciation of Music

III. Social and Academic Music Clubs which unify the music students and provide for them special opportunities to grow in the areas where they are specially gifted. Also, such clubs provide a means by which the music student may support interschool music festivals, publicize and support school concerts, and bring to the attention of the general student body seasonal celebrations and occasions of national commemoration, such as "American Education Week."

In conclusion, it should be noted that high school educators generally hold that (1) no education is truly complete without music; (2) the inclusion of music on the same basis as other subjects does not overcrowd the curriculum, but rather enriches every phase of school life, promoting happiness and creating a desire to find its complement in other school subjects, giving new life to old things and making real and near at hand those things that were unknown and far away; (3) education is more than an accumulation of knowledge, more than the training of a well-disciplined mind—it is training in the appreciation and understanding of things of value; and (4) the union of school with life outside is the goal sought today by all prominent educators.

They recognize music as one of the best tie-ups with the home and outside life.

Questions and Exercises

1. Would "democratic" be a good substitute for "progressive" in the term "progressive philosophy of education"? Why?
2. What is the place of music in the high school?
3. Are the values of music in the high school only immediate?
4. What other measures of a subject's curricular validity are there besides "satisfaction now"?
5. In reading the material under "Educational Applications" what did you find pertinent to your own high school experiences?
6. What should be the main objectives in the "general music" or "appreciation" class?
7. What are some measures of success in the "appreciation classes"?
8. Submit a complete coverage of the music offering in a high school, touching upon its philosophy and objectives; the curricular content; the agencies for carrying out the music program; the procedures for getting the job done; the fitting of music and the music teacher into the affairs of the school and the community.

Chapter 7

SOME NEEDS FOR PUBLIC MUSIC
EDUCATION TODAY

If education is to be effective at all, it must satisfy the felt
needs of the individual and in such a way as to prepare the
individual most effectively for the demands that will confront him in the future. It is apparent that the demands of
our life have been seriously beyond our ability to meet them,
indicating that our education thus far has been detached
from reality and, consequently, woefully inadequate. It is
our desperate need, then, to find and furnish more effective
education; and we are convinced that among the many bul-
warks of such education, music is one that we cannot afford
to overlook.

It is observable that music serves the needs of a large
number of persons, and that it deserves its sure place
in public education. It is one of the values which hardly
any thoughtful person will dare to neglect. But even though
the music educator has an important and respected position
in education, he must remember that in order to increase
the effectiveness of the music-education program it will be
necessary (1) to provide a greater quantity of a better
standard of music in our educational offering, and (2) to
improve the musicianship and the teaching ability of many
of the people teaching music who have only fulfilled the
too low minimum requirements for their music-teaching
"credentials" or "certificates." The need for increased musicianship of our music teachers carries with it the impera-

tive that we have better training programs for prospective music teachers.[1]

Development of Teachers' Musicianship

There are several curious sets of circumstances that hamper the development of teachers' musicianship. There is the difficulty of vocational placement for a good music teacher in some school systems. A teacher who has prepared himself educationally and musically for teaching finds that he has had little time to prepare himself (nor does he have much inclination to do so) for teaching subjects other than music. Yet many superintendents find themselves compelled to hire a teacher who can "handle" music along with one or two other subjects, all only moderately well, in preference to hiring a musician who is an expert teacher and who prefers to confine himself mostly to teaching music. Such a practice as this—to which superintendents find themselves economically driven—evidences a greater interest in the budget than in the children or the future of our citizenry.

The unfortunate consequences of employing music teachers who also teach other subjects are fourfold: (1) a full offering in music designed to satisfy the needs of all the children can scarcely be provided; (2) a teacher who divides his attention among several fields does not keep up adequately in music (which is in itself a diversified field); (3) a person who would prepare himself for music teaching recognizes that he must prepare to teach in areas other than

---

[1] This statement of needs is not to be construed as a pessimistic note, nor as a censorious criticism, nor as a strange contradiction of our usual pride in the achievements of the music educators of the land. While there are hundreds of places (as has already been suggested in Chapter 1) where wonderful things are being done in music education, there are also hundreds of communities where inadequate or shockingly poor work is being done.

in music if he is to make a living, and therefore in the first place does not even attempt to gain much more than a minimum training for music teaching; (4) a person who could become a fine teacher of music, recognizing that he would have to compromise his musical ideals, may go into another field altogether, keeping music to himself for strictly private and avocational enjoyment.

Dangers in a Diversified Teaching Load. There are other factors besides those of vocational placement which tend to discourage music-teaching specialization and which, therefore, make it difficult to provide adequate music experiences for school children. The consequent conditions are especially clear at the elementary level. In general, the elementary school teacher has to teach nearly all subjects in the curriculum: art, physical education, music, nutrition, hygiene, social responsibility, English, even a foreign language sometimes, arithmetic, reading, penmanship, history, citizenship, civic institutions, crafts—altogether something like twenty-two fields in which the teacher is expected to be expert.[2] Now it is conceivable that one teacher could satisfactorily handle the integrating and the teaching of such subjects as language, reading, writing, arithmetic, history, and social responsibility and citizenship, but surely that would be enough for one person—without expecting him to teach in the specialized fields (such as art, physical education, and music) which are so necessary for the full nurturing of children and which can hardly be taught in any way but harmfully by a person inexpert in those fields. Yet in

[2] What we have is a condition in which either good music teachers are teaching general subjects along with music or else general teachers are assigned to teach the special subjects (art, music, etc.) along with their regular subjects. This may satisfy the official requirements of a curriculum committee's recommendation or a state's requirement, but it will not satisfy educational responsibility to the child.

many places it is common practice for the general teacher to be carrying the full load in the special fields too.

This spreading thin of a teacher's acquaintance with his teaching fields is the result of a view in some systems that children of elementary school age should be guided and taught only by one teacher in order for them to have a warmth of affection and trust toward their teacher such as a child should have toward his parents. The values in such a view are often mostly imaginary. However, there is no educational malfeasance in employing special teachers to work with the general teachers by visiting them and teaching their children in those special areas which deserve and must have such expert support. Nor is such a practice of having supplementary specialized teaching, which is common in many culturally advanced places, proportionately out of line in terms of expense. Of course it has been a general practice in many places to have supervisors aid the general teacher in the specialized areas. This practice is even more economical. But as has already been indicated, many underprivileged areas cannot afford even the supervisorial services.

Surely it need not be pointed out here that too little money is spent on teachers and on education generally. Indeed, the reasons why schools in general do not accomplish what they would like and what they could are to be found in inadequate financing; the spreading too thin of the training of teachers; the hiring of too few teachers for the job; the hiring of inadequately prepared teachers; and the scheduling of too diverse teaching assignments to the teachers. In reference to music, there are, in altogether too many instances, good music teachers who cannot get a music-teaching job but who instead must diversify their teaching to an educationally dangerous degree; or else the practice is to assign music-teaching jobs of gravest responsi-

bility to people with inadequate or even no musical training. Such bad practice must be remedied if we are to avoid
great harm to the children.

Satisfaction of Children's Musical Needs. In many places
today the natural musical needs of children are not being
sensitively and carefully nurtured. All too often, a *dislike*
erroneously directed toward *real* music is fostered in the
children's hearts because the claptrap that ill-prepared
teachers present to the children is being passed off as music.
The developing of the potential which resides in most children to utilize music creatively for their own sensitive
growth is being neglected, especially on the elementary
level.

This is also true on the secondary level, and here the condition is even more cancerous because, while orchestras,
bands, and choruses are actually organized and encouraged,
they are given largely to preparing "musical" exhibits conducted by teaching artisans who can handle the technical
details of musical performance fairly well but are actually
unaware of the profound responsibilities of musical education.[3] If the teachers were not so unaware of the deeper
aspects of their work, so many of them would not be caught
in, or at least be so lackadaisical about, the frivolous music-
education system in which many of them operate.

It is the failure to develop in children, and in teachers, a
creative sensitivity to music that made possible the profound observation by a visitor to one of our music confer-
ences when he said that he had never heard so much bad
music played so expertly.

---

[3] There is an interesting consequence to all this: the considerable lack of
musical "carry-over" from school life to adult life. Upon becoming adult,
many school musicians have lost interest in music activities which were not
really musical, but, rather, gregarious—that is, tending to develop loyalty
to the school, not developing love for music.

Significant Experiences with Good Music

There will be many who will ask why it is important to have children become acquainted with good music, expertly presented. All too often music is thought of merely as a filler of spare time. Music educators must make it known that the values in musical experiences will be only superficial ones if those experiences are completely confined to pleasing the relatives who come to hear their children play in a concert, or to pleasing the populace at a football game. Such utilitarian and associative values are important, but they are not the *real* values of music in education.

Good music, at whatever level—popular, "semiclassical," or serious—as it manifests its degree of goodness in terms of being liked by people, must for each individual be a constantly changing music advancing steadily toward constantly improved quality. People who use music on the same level soon tire of it, and if they have not learned to advance in their use and apprehension of music, they sooner or later discard that music as a source of satisfaction, and, finally, discard all music as a serious source of satisfaction. Such regrettable discarding results in the building of tensions, the creating of emptiness and boredom, the frustrating of purposes and vision, and the stultifying of sensitivity. The more advanced the quality of the music and the more able the person who apprehends it, the more deeply will that person be transformed as he experiences such music.

An Authentic Musical Offering

Thus music educators desire that music be taught by *adequately prepared* music teachers who *love children* and who *love good music*; and that the music offering in the schools be complete and significant and of a high standard.

The ideal would be for every elementary school to have available a sufficient number of teaching musicians to reach every class in the school twice a week and, in addition, to provide choral and orchestral and class instrumental teaching for all who are qualified to profit from such instruction. If the teachers are scheduled efficiently, special instructors can individually service several schools in their respective specialties, all this amounting to no more than the equivalent of one music teacher per building.

In the junior and senior high schools, at least chorus, orchestra, band, instrumental classes, and music appreciation courses should be available. These should be taught by music-teaching specialists. In the senior high schools additional musical offerings might well be contemplated.

There is no substitute for beautiful music performed beautifully for the enjoyment of the performers and for the delight of sensitive, well-educated hearers.

Questions and Exercises

1. Should general teachers teach music in the schools? Should only "special" music teachers be allowed to teach music? Should a cooperative teaching of music by general and special teachers under competent music supervision be the practice?
2. Does the phrase "teaching a child within the framework of his experience-based comprehension" mean that the music quality must be brought down to the child's level of "appreciation"?
3. Select several popular compositions and also several serious compositions and examine them for their marks of craftsmanship.
4. How has education of yesteryear failed the present generation?
5. What is beneficial about popular music? What damaging?

6. Are the inadequate qualifications of music teachers due to economic or philosophic circumstances? (We do not refer necessarily to what is said in this chapter, but rather to what your own experience and thinking indicate.)
7. Do you agree that musicianship of teachers needs desperately to be improved?
8. Do you feel that the steps necessary for improvement could readily be taken?

Chapter 8

MUSIC IN THE COLLEGE

While the musical objectives in elementary and secondary schools have been carefully defined and widely published by music educators, the aims for music in the liberal
arts colleges have for the most part been stated only
vaguely; and where clearer statements have been attempted,
they are in total disagreement with one another.

Liberal arts colleges are peculiarly individualistic even
though they recognize that an attempt should be made to
standardize[1] their offerings. This individualism arises out
of their being founded for different purposes in religion,
educational method, and professional, vocational, and
scholarly achievement. The individualism also arises out of
their being established by people who differ inherently and
economically in abilities to establish a liberal arts college.

PRESENT STATUS OF MUSIC IN THE LIBERAL ARTS COLLEGE

Until recently the only readily available source of information as to the present status of music in the liberal arts
colleges has been Randall Thompson's report of 1935 based

[1] Even this notion of standardization is fraught with difficulty and ambi-
guity. In the realm of higher education, any Procrustean kind of standardization would be obnoxious. Yet the need to transfer credits, to appraise
them for graduate work, etc., requires some uniform attitude toward
accreditation.

Some liberal arts colleges hold that their offering is pre-vocational and
pre-professional; others that liberal arts education properly includes
teacher-training, business administration, etc.; some colleges emphasize the
humanities because their constituency is economically privileged, while
"grass roots" colleges may include vocational and avocational work in order
better to serve their constituency. Berea College and Antioch College provide interesting offerings.

on the findings of a serious committee study of college curricula directed by Ernest Hatch Wilkins, president of Oberlin College. This committee secured the services of Randall Thompson, who visited more than thirty representative liberal arts colleges all over the country.[2]

It should be noted that the report was based on a study made during 1932–33 and was published in 1935. The task of carrying on such a study was a formidable one, so much so that perhaps it will be some time before another one of such a kind is attempted.[3] The investigation was a cross-section study of a changing, fluctuating educational offering, and thus the factual findings are not to be considered a very close approximation of the status of music in the liberal arts colleges today. However, several important conclusions that were deduced from the study are probably still true at the present time. In his report, Randall Thompson asserts that the day for defending music's position in colleges is past and that all educators recognize that music has a place in liberal arts college education.

During the present century, college music has grown in two directions: (1) in the direction of the establishment of a department of music offering a major in music toward the B.A. degree, and (2) in the direction of a school or conservatory of music offering the B. Mus. degree. In this latter direction, where the school or conservatory of music has been established, an added responsibility has been assumed by the music school or department: that of providing vocational and professional training in music along with providing for the musical needs of students of other departments.

[2] Among them were the following institutions: Amherst, Barnard, Baylor, Bethany, Bryn Mawr, Carleton, Centenary, Chicago, Columbia, Converse, Cornell, Fisk, Grinnell, Harvard, Iowa, Michigan, Mills, Newcomb, North Carolina, Oberlin, Oregon, Pomona, Radcliffe, St. Olaf, Smith, Syracuse, Vassar, Virginia, Wellesley, and Yale.

[3] See Tables at end of chapter for recent data collected and tabulated by the author.

There has also been a third plan under which a private school of music, independent of the college, has been taken into an arrangement whereby the independent school provides professional training, the college provides academic training, and one institution or the other, or both, then award degrees either in music or in arts. Such an independent but cooperative arrangement usually eliminates the necessity of establishing a music faculty in the college—or at most the college will need to provide only a very small number of music teachers. Early in their history, the University of Michigan and the School of Music at Ann Arbor, and Oberlin College and the Oberlin Conservatory of Music were independent of each other; later on, in both cases, they became organically affiliated.

In the study made by Randall Thompson it is noted that in the colleges which were visited the proportion of work in music counted toward the B.A. degree might be as great as 56 per cent. Usually, though, only 30 to 40 per cent of the work required for the degree was in music and the balance was in other academic subjects or fields.

Another point of deviation in the music offerings of liberal arts colleges is bound up with the various educators' attitudes toward the value of applied music as a part of the music curriculum. Generally speaking, music history, music theory, and music appreciation are universally offered and accepted as curricular study toward the B.A. degree. But considerable differences of opinion have arisen, both among educators in fields other than music and also among the music educators themselves, as to crediting applied music. These differences have arisen chiefly over whether or not to recognize performance in singing or on an instrument as being a suitable college subject. And when learning to perform *is* regarded as a suitable college subject, difficulty arises over determining a method of evaluating it and determining its "credit worth." Thus, there is little unanimity as to the question of how to have similar college degrees represent at least approximately equivalent value. The Music Teachers National Association and the National Association of Schools of Music are working on the problem of reconciling such differences.

The reasons that are given by some colleges for including applied music for credit are the very reasons that are given by others for excluding applied music: (1) Some assert that performing music is a skill and so should—or should not!— be credited toward the B.A. (2) Some take the attitude that musical performance develops the mind. Others deny that it develops the mind. (3) Some are certain that music performance is easily measured. Others are sure that no one can measure what, if any, musical ability is included in musical performance.

Among many examples from Randall Thompson's study these are interesting: Harvard allows no credit for applied music, Iowa allows 21.7 per cent of the college work toward the B.A. to be in applied music, Michigan allows 10 per cent, Oberlin 8.1 per cent.[4]

Another type of applied music is offered in most colleges, namely, "class instruction and group participation." Under this heading there are choirs, choruses, glee clubs, bands, orchestras, and miscellaneous combinations of vocal or instrumental groups, and instructional class lessons in group performance techniques.

The number of ways devised for giving credit for group music participation is legion. In the class lessons in techniques the value is usually computed just as that of any other academic course. Sometimes, however, credit in the

[4] What happens, of course, as a result of all this variation is that a student who considers musical performance as a part of life's delights and who wishes to study applied music further will refrain from going to Harvard or to any other institution that will not give him what he most desires.

class is dependent upon participation in one of the campus music organizations.

There are obvious disadvantages attending group teaching of applied music techniques: (1) Poor students in a class of unequal students hold the good ones back. (2) If the class is small it is very expensive (because students do not pay a special fee for special attention); if it is large it is inefficient, for there is little or no time to help with individual difficulties. (3) Group instruction cuts down on departmental income, thus eventually eliminating teachers.

But there are advantages too: (1) Reduction in the staff is a saving to the college. (2) A reduction in cost makes music lessons available to more students. (3) An instructor can cover ground with a group in one meeting that in private lessons would necessitate much repetition of his work. (4) Social advantages and opportunities are helpful to the student in learning to prepare himself for public performance. (5) Fellowship and a certain amount of competition are desirable elements in group lessons. (6) The less gifted student profits by the example of the gifted.

Credit for private instruction in units or semester hours, where credit is awarded, is usually based on one or the other of two plans: (1) two half-hours per week (sometimes one sixty-minute lesson) and one hour of daily practice are awarded one semester hour of credit; (2) in other colleges the same amount of work is given two semester hours of credit. (This latter is recommended by the National Association of Schools of Music.)

In a liberal arts college, with the trend toward vocational training, especially in those colleges offering teacher training and commercial and business administration preparation, music faces two possibilities: it may be included in the curriculum either for avocational purposes or for vocational training.

Vocational Considerations

If music in the liberal arts college curriculum serves the vocational needs of many of the students, it will generally be along the lines of preparation for music teaching in schools. It would seem that such preparation in the liberal arts college should be broad enough to include the same spread of fields of learning as any other major—as in the case of English, for example. But with such general academic preparation the student thus prepared for school music-teaching is often not sufficiently prepared musically, even with the equivalent of sixty semester hours of credit in music. (Sixty hours is rarely allowed for the B.A. degree, although with careful choices of electives it could be worked in. However, many schools limit the proportion to 45 semester hours or less. For example, Bradley University has limited the work in music toward a B.A. degree to 45 hours, and required 84 semester hours as a minimum in other areas. Bradley is a member of the North Central Association and of the National Association of Schools of Music.)

It must be remembered that more often than not, the music student in college has to spend considerable time in learning about the tools of his subject, such as music syntax, music reading, music writing, and music performing. This is not true of other major pursuits in college so far as tools are concerned. In short, the music student who is ready to graduate from a liberal arts college with sixty semester hours of music is just near to being on a par with other college students about to declare their major in, say, English at the beginning of the junior year. Thus one might suggest that the music major who is preparing vocationally for teaching should carry on concentrated musical study during a fifth year, and then prepare for an M.A. in the sixth year, unless the musical preparation during pre-college days has been very highly developed, which is not often the case.

Liberal arts colleges often contend that music students with vocational objectives in mind should go to a music school and study toward a B. Mus. degree. Although this may be desirable in certain instances, it defeats the general purpose of liberal arts college education. Vocationally, then, music in the liberal arts college of today presents this dilemma: (1) the average music major sequence of studies in a regular liberal arts college curriculum does not give the student adequate musical preparation; (2) an adequate musical preparation as offered by some liberal arts colleges does not give the student sufficient experience in the general curriculum that a liberal arts college is supposed to provide; (3) a student is not being adequately compensated when he does the extra work in order to prepare himself culturally and professionally and is then paid the same salary for six years of preparation plus considerable childhood special preparation as a student with an academic M.A. As a consequence some liberal arts colleges have felt it unwise to encourage music students vocationally, even while recognizing that there is a tremendous need for music teachers and that the demands of living require that we have music teachers with broad educational experiences.

Thus, several possible curricular plans present themselves: (1) A curriculum in professional schools of music leading to the B. Mus. degree and including sufficient general cultural experience. Since such a course of study would extend through several years, it should come to be recognized as vocationally deserving of a satisfactory and professionally remunerative stipend. (2) A regular liberal arts college preparation leading to the B.A. degree, including in music the proportion of credit hours usually allotted to the major. The content of such a course is to be considered as a *pre-*

professional music training. Professional music study should
follow later and accordingly be awarded suitable professional recognition. An important objection to this plan is
that advanced musical study is delayed too long. Some
schools under such a plan require their students to pass a
performance examination although their outside study and
preparation for performance (applied music) are not allowed as credit in their collegiate course. This is an unpop-
ular arrangement with many music students. (3) A liberal
arts college curriculum that includes sufficient music in an
altogether different kind of course leading to the B.A. degree. In such a plan, which marks a radical departure from
tradition, courses would be proportioned much as in custom-
ary sequences leading to the B.M. or B.M.Ed. degrees. Traditional requirements in the natural sciences, social sciences,
and similar fields would be considered as partially substi-
tuted for through courses in music history, citizenship, philosophy, and esthetics. Knowledge of the scientific methods
would be efficiently provided through study in philosophy
and educational psychology.

Such a new offering would contribute more directly to
the music student's interests and needs; it would contribute
to his vocational preparation with no lessening of orientation in the humanities and the sciences.[5]

[5] There are many who ask if the traditional liberal arts college curricula
are not actually just pre-law or pre-medicine or pre-professional training
after all, although offered under the guise of being liberal arts programs. It
is felt by many that such professional preparation as found in pre-medical
courses has been proved valid historically in a liberal arts curriculum, and
that therefore teacher training and music training can be added legitimately
to the list of pre-professional offerings usually found in the liberal arts college. These querists feel that the opposition to music training and teacher
training comes from departments that would no longer have their courses
required of *all* students in the proposed enlarged offering. These are the
ones who, it is felt by some, insist that their courses are cultural and tradi-
tionally liberal when actually they are just pre-professional courses although
of long historical standing.

A fourth plan, which is in accord with the recommendations of the Research Council of the Music Educators National Conference, is to have the liberal arts college—if it is adequately equipped and staffed—offer a sufficient concentration in music and pedagogical subjects (about three-fourths); and a portion in English, physical education, philosophy, and citizenship (one-fourth): the graduate to be awarded, upon satisfactory completion of the requirements, the B. Mus. or B. Mus. Ed. degree. Such a program would assure at least fair musical preparation, an acquaintance with the tools of living, and some appreciation of the scientific method, love for learning, and a responsible attitude toward citizenship in the light of history.

AVOCATIONAL CONSIDERATIONS

As has already been mentioned, the day for defending music's place as a legitimate part of the humanities in the college curriculum is past. The problems now connected with its inclusion have to do with the *means* and the *how* of teaching music in the liberal arts college. These are determined largely by the location of the college, the type of student, the nature of the community served, and the size of the institution, its income, equipment, and its faculty.

Generally the aims of college music have been to provide the opportunity to acquire (1) more general appreciation, (2) more general knowledge, (3) musical scholarship, and (4) skill in musical composition. However, the latter two are usually not emphasized in liberal arts college education.

So far as the curriculum for avocational use of music is concerned (to satisfy the liberalizing purposes of the music department), the subject fields of music history, music appreciation, music theory, and, in some colleges, applied music have been considered sufficient. It has been found that students majoring in other departments do well in electives such as music theory and music history. Thus, in general, no student is "ruled out" from taking music courses.[6]

However, in recent years, with the increasing appreciation for music's place in the liberal arts college, educators have regarded it more and more necessary to provide, for the general student who may have only a casual interest in music, an environment that includes rich musical experiences. For this reason and on this basis, concerts by artists are arranged for, opportunities for musical performances by students in concerts and in general assemblies are provided, opportunity for community singing in general assembly is often planned, participation in one or more of the college musical organizations is often available, and the opportunity to study music history or music theory of course is open to all. Some of these offerings are considered to be curricular (that is, valid for receiving credit) in certain colleges, extracurricular (noncredit) in others. A number of colleges endeavor to integrate their music with the work in other fields, for instance, as with the work in an all-embracing "humanities course."

DEMOCRATIC EDUCATIONAL IDEALS

In this section specific recommendations will be made for utilizing music as a functionalistic agency in the liberal arts college curriculum. Little has been done toward attempting to establish functionalism in the curricula of the colleges of the land.

[6] It has been pointed out that even in the private study of performance, the general student frequently does as well as the student studying music vocationally. *Conference on Music in Liberal Arts College* (Oberlin: Music Teachers National Association, 1935), p. 22.

Functionalism embodies pragmatism as a method, if not as a philosophy, and the maxim of the method has been: "We learn to do by doing." As stated previously, there are certain pitfalls that are likely to confront the person who adopts the maxim as his "rule of faith and practice." *What* one does has a great deal to do with what one *learns*.[7] On this very score, the essentialists have opposed the pragmatists. They have said, in effect, that the progressive activities have been aimless, desultory, misguided, and unfruitful. Because the activities have been badly chosen, and have also been given the "highest place"—so the enemies of progressivism have charged—the concept of democracy, instead of being strengthened, has been developed into a still farther reach of anarchy, of irresponsible individualism, involving at least a lack of respect for teamwork, if not the absolute violation of other persons' rights.

The main criticism of progressivism has actually been brought about because of a much-needed attack against those who misunderstand the pragmatic method or are unable to utilize the pragmatic method in their own personal way of teaching.

One is confronted with these questions: Can and should the curricula of liberal arts colleges be established on the "area of experience" or "progressive" basis? Or should the "subject-of-study" system be retained with adaptations that will utilize the pragmatic method of teaching in so far as is possible?

Since all the phases of music that are likely to be taught in colleges—whether they be subjects such as history or theory, or activities such as piano playing or choral singing—have values that lend themselves readily to the essentialistic, the traditionalistic, or the pragmatic methods, surely no

[7] See discussion of progressive education on pp. 80–84.

special harm will come from presenting music at first as a field of "subjects." The task will therefore fall upon the teacher to present music in the best way possible in the light of his philosophical and pedagogical attitude toward education.

Of course, many have felt that drastic changes in liberal arts college philosophy are imperative. Many believe that education between adolescence and maturity must be more practical and more liberal, and that colleges must abandon attempts to prepare students professionally. Rather, they believe that the student should be aroused intellectually by opening up broad vistas of scientific and social potentialities.[8]

Ross L. Finney is one who has been emphatic in declaring that the liberal arts colleges must train leaders. He has asserted that the constants in liberal arts college curricula must be science, fine arts, and the new humanities; and that the electives must be such subjects as mathematics, formal English, and foreign languages.[9]

At any rate certain terms well known in the general educator's vocabulary imply processes that can easily be adopted by the music teacher regardless of his traditional pedagogy. Such words as *correlation, integration, functionalism,* and *articulation* can readily be taken into the vocabulary of the college music teacher. *Activities* certainly can be nowhere more at home than in the performance of music.

In fact, the whole problem of a consistent inclusion of applied music in liberal arts college curricula might seem now to be related to the struggle and misunderstanding

[8] Norman Woefel, *Molders of the American Mind* (New York: Columbia University Press, 1933), p. 123.
[9] Ross L. Finney, *A Sociological Philosophy of Education* (New York: The Macmillan Co., 1928), pp. 285, 290.

between essentialism and pragmatism or progressivism. Only a few liberal arts colleges have done very much toward finding what activities and areas of experience could do if made a part of their curricula. It is to be noted that the brunt of the attack against music as a part of the college curricula is directed against that phase of music which has to do with actual performance; and that the part which is pretty generally acceptable is the phase that often embodies dull, tedious lectures during a predetermined period of time devoted to learning *about* music.

Those persons who disapprove of accrediting "applied music" do so on the basis that it is mostly activity and seldom musical "learning"—that it therefore does not fit in with the basic purpose of liberal arts college education, namely, enriching the store of cultural knowledge as gained from (1) observation, (2) study, (3) *logical* thinking, and (4) research. Perhaps the basic purpose of liberal arts college education would be better served by insisting on the curricular addition of (5) *planned experiences and activities* satisfying human needs.

Therefore, to complete a listing of music offerings in a progressivistic liberal arts college, working on the subject basis, the following should be included:

1. Every student desiring to participate in some sort of musical organization, such as men's chorus, women's chorus, mixed chorus, band, orchestra, or string quartet, should have the opportunity. The problem involved here is made more difficult by *not banning anyone* from musical participation, whatever his ability. In general, liberal arts colleges provide musical opportunity only to those who are to some extent gifted. Although expense is entailed by having several musical organizations, sufficient musical

activity should be provided to serve all who desire it. Laboratory credit should be awarded for such activity.[10]

2. Every student who so desires and has the ability should have the opportunity to participate in some fine music organization built upon the selective basis. Such groups should be available for both singing and playing. They, also, should earn laboratory credit.

3. Opportunity should be provided for students to hear concerts by other students and by artists either at a reasonable charge or entirely free of charge. A general assembly should sometimes be scheduled, at which, among other things, opportunity would be provided for singing community songs and perhaps hymns.

4. Opportunity should be provided for the election of courses in history or theory, or for enrollment in applied music. Such music offerings should be open to all who are qualified.

It is interesting to note that courses in music history and music theory are offered in the most conservative of liberal arts colleges without question, although they are least likely to be well taught. Classes in music history should be closely correlated with social studies, with musical participation

---

[10] By "laboratory" credit is meant credit given on the same basis as that given for science laboratory periods. Persons earning credit in an organization should be satisfactory members and should learn group music technique. One way to gain a knowledge of group technique is for the instructor to have informal small groups perform special selections for the larger group, after which an opportunity for discussion and questions is provided. If some students wish, instead of achieving accomplished performance, they might be permitted to submit a creditable 2,000-word paper on some phase of music touched upon by the organization during the year. (The paper might be allowed as a theme in one of the English classes.) No credit should be given for less than one year's participation. Each group should make one or more creditable performances (depending upon the organization) before the student body (or a selected group from the student body) in either general assembly or formal concert.

and performance, and with literature; and certain portions of music history should be correlated with philosophy, physics and acoustics, and mathematics. The courses in music history and appreciation offered in colleges that are close to community centers where fine artist appearances are available to the public might well relate their course-content to the public concerts during the music season. Preparation in class for a gala trip to the concert and a late-evening "supper discussion" afterward is one of the best kinds of music education.

The work in music theory should include considerable original composition, and it should not of course be restricted for two years to four-part hymn tunes. Such theory classes might well contribute toward the writing of songs for various special occasions, school songs, and other musical pieces, the better ones to be presented in general assembly or in special recital performances.

A general overhauling is needed badly in the classes in theory and sight singing.[11] It might be added that college instructors would do well to take a leaf out of the elementary school music teacher's book.

Opportunity should be provided the students to learn to perform, by enrolling either for private lessons or class lessons in singing or playing. Credit for these should include requirements similar to group performance requirements, as stated before, plus sufficient outside practice. One hour of lesson time plus ten to twelve hours of outside practice per week, plus certain other requirements such as writing assignments would earn four hours of credit; two

[11] There is a decided trend all over the country toward combining sight singing, ear training, terminology, written harmony, keyboard harmony, and elementary form and composition into a single integrated course, the class meeting five times a week under the same instructor, each class period including a well-balanced combination of all the different kinds of work, and the prime objective of the entire course being *musicianship*.

hours of credit would be earned by carrying just half such a load.

5. Opportunity should be provided to engage in special activities that would vitalize the community life of a college campus. College music educators should not overlook the possibility of using the members of the general faculty or the faculty wives, or the other adult members of the non-college community. All of these might very well fit into the college musical program as a nucleus for orchestra, chorus, or instrumental groups.

The members of the faculty should be admitted at nominal charges, or even free, to the artist-concerts and to the other musical activities of the college. This would help to educate the general faculty into a healthful music awareness. Students should be admitted to the artist-concerts at a low rate. Usually an activity card arrangement for providing low-priced concert admission works best. Some colleges present artists of highest musical renown for as little as an eight-cent charge to the student. Such fees are best prepaid upon registration at which time the student receives his activity card admitting him without further charge to all college events.

Concert standards and quality of music need never be lowered in order to hold the interest of students. That has been demonstrated time and time again on numbers of campuses. College students want the best there is.

There is another musical activity of great value to both the general student and music student. This is a sort of intramural competition that may go on throughout the college year in the fields of music, art, drama, literature, and home arts. Both creativity and performance are judged in each of the fields. Students entering the competition appear or exhibit before the student body and before a competent judging committee. The work is scored from event to event throughout the year. At the end of the year, a sweepstakes winner, and a first, second, and third place winner in each area of endeavor are announced. Certificates and trophies may be awarded.

6. For those who desire it, opportunity should be provided to prepare one's self either vocationally or avocationally in the music department of a liberal arts college. However, the vocational objective should not be overemphasized in the B.A. sequence, and should be offered only if the school is adequately equipped for it, and only to the extent of preparing the student to do later university graduate work in music as a profession.

While the liberal arts college should provide basic experience that will prepare the talented or qualified student for further vocational study, the *primary* function of the liberal arts college music department should be to provide (1) a musical environment, (2) opportunity for musical participation, and (3) a sufficient offering for the avocational pursuit of music, toward the end that the college student may be prepared to derive deep satisfaction from music as a collegiate subject and as a post-collegiate source of happiness.

There has been much effort expended in order to serve the general college student who may have no vocational interest in music. Courses for such students usually are referred to as music appreciation courses. The teachers often require of enrolled general students a considerable concentrated listening to recordings, and the developing of a recognition repertoire of basic compositions. An appreciation of music does not necessarily spring out of such courses, although when skillfully conducted, they are very often quite popular.

Perhaps a greater appreciation of music and the power to gain satisfaction from music grow out of actual performance, such as in choral and instrumental ensembles, no matter how elementary such activity and performance may be (so long as it is centered around music of fine quality). Indeed the listening-to-records lesson is only one of many approaches to appreciation, as has been pointed out in previous chapters. (See pp. 48, 64, 88–92.) The listening lesson while very important and, at first appearance, seemingly the easiest to prepare and present, is perhaps the most difficult to teach successfully. This is partly because the pupil as a listener is likely to be more nearly passive than in any other kind of musical experience. It is observable that any teaching objective, if it is to be realized, must be attached to significant experiences within the framework of the pupil's ready comprehension. Ben Jonson said, "What care I how simple it be, if it be not ever so simple to me."

One of the problems treated throughout this volume is how to develop appreciation for music. Successful solution of this problem is dependent upon numerous educational and musical processes. Music appreciation is not just a compartment in music education—rather, it is the very essence and fulfillment of music education.

TABLE 1

Music Offering	No. of Colleges
No music	17
Music activity only *	60
Music activity and some courses	90
Minor for the following degrees:	
Bachelor of Arts	19
Bachelor of Education	2
Bachelor of Science	11
Bachelor of Science in Education	1
Master of Arts	2
Major for the following degrees:	
Bachelor of Arts	433
Bachelor of Arts in Education	12
Bachelor of Arts in Music Education	6
Bachelor of Education	8
Bachelor of Fine Arts	11
Bachelor of Fine Arts in Education	3
Bachelor of Music	165
Bachelor of Music—Major in Music Education	14
Bachelor of Music Education	70
Bachelor of Philosophy	1
Bachelor of Sacred Music	1
Bachelor of School Music	2
Bachelor of Science	61
Bachelor of Science—Major in Music Education	5
Bachelor of Science in Education	45
Bachelor of Science in Music Education	31
Master of Arts	61
Master of Arts in Education of Music	4
Master of Education	4
Master of Fine Arts	4
Master of Music	37
Master of Music—Major in Music Education	5
Master of Music Education	10
Master of Science	3
Master of Science—Major in Music Education	3
Minister of Music	1
Doctor of Education	3
Doctor of Philosophy	11
Total number of colleges in the United States †	1,134
Total number of colleges that responded to survey (1949–50)	723
Percentage of colleges that responded to survey (1949–50).	63.7%

* † See following page for notes.

Because colleges frequently offer more than one degree, the sum of the college offerings is greater than the number of colleges that responded to survey.

TABLE 2

Music Offering	No. of Junior Colleges
No music	11
Music activity only *	23
Music activity and some courses	75
College Preparatory—no degree	4
Associate in Music	3
Associate in Science	4
Associate of Arts:	
College Preparatory	57
Junior College Terminal	49
Associate of Fine Arts	2
Certificate of Efficiency	1
Certificate of Fine Arts	3
Certificate of Graduation	1
Certificate of Music	2
Junior Certificate	1
Diploma	30
Fine Arts Diploma	1
Junior College Diploma—minor only	5
Does not indicate degree	2
Total number of junior colleges in the United States †.....	495
Total number of junior colleges that responded to survey (1949–50)	244
Percentage of junior colleges that responded to survey (1949–50)	49.3%

* This includes bands, orchestras, choral groups, quartets, glee clubs, instrumental and vocal ensembles.

† This total is based on the 1949–50 Educational Directory of the United States Office of Education.

TABLE 3

VARIATION IN PRIVATE MUSIC INSTRUCTION OFFERINGS IN THE
COLLEGES AND UNIVERSITIES, STATE TEACHERS COLLEGES
AND JUNIOR COLLEGES

Schools offering no private instruction	Colleges and Universities	(61)
	Teachers Colleges	(21)
	Junior Colleges	(36)
Schools offering private instruction but allowing no credit	Colleges and Universities	(29)
	Teachers Colleges	(14)
	Junior Colleges	(22)
Schools offering private instruction with credit	Colleges and Universities	(271)
	Teachers Colleges	(75)
	Junior Colleges	(80)
Schools offering private instruction both with and without credit	Colleges and Universities	(66)
	Teachers Colleges	(4)
	Junior Colleges	(15)

	Colleges and Universities	Teachers Colleges	Junior Colleges
Total number of schools in the United States *	924	210	495
Total number of schools that responded to survey (1949–50)	427	114	153
Percentage of schools that responded to survey (1949–50)	46%	54%	30%

* This total is based on the 1949–50 Educational Directory of the United States Office of Education.

TABLE 4

Status of Musical Experience as a Requirement for Graduation
from Colleges and Universities, State Teachers
Colleges, and Junior Colleges

Musical Experience	Colleges and Universities	Teachers Colleges	Junior Colleges
No answer	19	4	11
Do not require musical experience	309	40	119
Do require musical experience	99	70	23
Description of musical experience required:			
Music Appreciation	9	8	3
Music or Art	11	3	2
Music, Art, or Drama	1		
Music Theory and Methods		3	
Fine Arts	9	1	
Humanities	2		
Polish Music			1
Public School Music			1
Teacher Training Curriculum		2	3
Elementary Education Curriculum		5	
Class Piano for Kindergarten-Primary Curriculum		1	
Liberal Arts Curriculum	4		
Participation in Music Organizations (Chorus, orchestra, band, etc.)	3		
Assembly Singing			1
Liturgical Singing			1
Attendance at Concerts	1		
Not Indicated	59	47	11
Total number of schools in the United States *	924	210	495
Total number of schools that responded to survey (1949–50)	427	114	153
Percentage of schools that responded to survey (1949–50)	46%	54%	30%

* This total is based on the 1949–50 Educational Directory of the United States Office of Education.

TABLE 5

TABULATION AND CLASSIFICATION OF PRIVATE MUSIC INSTRUCTION FOR CREDIT AS OFFERED IN 346 COLLEGES, UNIVERSITIES, AND STATE TEACHERS COLLEGES OUT OF 541 RESPONDING TO SURVEY

(Showing length and number of lessons, semester hours of credit, and hours of daily practice)

Semester Hours Credit Allowed / Lessons Given per Week		25-Min. Lessons (11 Colleges)						30-Min. Lessons (290 Colleges)										40-Min. (5 Colleges)			45-Min. (6 Colleges)				50-Min. (14 Colleges)				55-Min. (1)	60-Min. Lessons (30 Colleges)				
Credit*	Lessons	½	1	1½	2	5	No Req.	½	1	1½	2	2½	3	4	5	No Req.	No Ind.	1	1½	2	1	1½	2	3	1	1½	2	3	2	1	1½	2	3	4
2/9 hr.	One								1																									
1/3 hr.	One								2									1																
4/9 hr.	Two																																	
1/2 hr.	One								3		1					1											1				2			
2/3 hr.	One								26	1	1					2						1					1				4			
2/3 hr.	Two								4																									
1 hr.	One	3		1				3	105	3	10					6	3	2			1	1			4	1	4	1	1		7	5	1	
1 hr.	Two								12		4					1	1														2			
1 1/3 hr.	One								5	1	3																1				1			
1 1/3 hr.	Two								1	1	8																							
1 1/2 hr.	One								7											1														
1 1/2 hr.	Two																																	
2 hr.	One	2							27	6	7		1			1		2				1			4		4	2	1		7	5		
2 hr.	Two	2		1	2				30	11	46		5			4											1				2		2	
2 hr.	Three										1		1																		1			
2 hr.	Five					1											1																	
2 2/3 hr.	One										2																							
2 2/3 hr.	Two									2													1								4			
3 hr.	One								2																						1			
3 hr.	Two								9	21			7			2				1						1								
3 hr.	Three												1																					
3 1/3 hr.	Two									1																								
4 hr.	One								1		1																				1			
4 hr.	Two						1				15		14	4						1											2		2	
4 hr.	Three										1																							
5 hr.	One																		1													4		
5 hr.	Two					1							5	1																				
5 hr.	Five																																	
6 hr.	Two										1	7																			1			
8 hr.	Two																																	

Total number of colleges in the United States † 1124
Total number of colleges that responded to survey (1949–50) 541
Percentage of colleges that responded to survey (1949–50) 48%

* All credit has been adjusted to semester hour basis.
† This total is based on the 1949–50 Educational Directory of the United States Office of Education.

USE OF TABLES 5–8:

In the top line, under 30-minute lessons, we find one college requiring one hour of practice daily for 2/9 of a semester hour's credit; in the seventh line, under 40-minute lessons, we find two colleges requiring one hour of practice daily for one semester hour's credit.

Because almost all the colleges offer several variations in the four categories of our concern here—namely, length of lessons, number of lessons, credit allowed, and practice required—the totals of any column or row on the table will never agree with the number of colleges.

In Table 5 there are 290 colleges of those in the United States replying to the survey which offer 30-minute lessons; one which offers 55 minute lessons. Nine colleges do not specify a time limit on lessons.

NOTE: A college which offers lessons of differing lengths of time will be classified several times, once under each column representing the length of lesson which the college offers.

Of the 541 colleges replying, the general practice seems to be to offer one semester hour of credit for one 30-minute lesson per week and require on hour of daily practice. In another widely accepted plan, two semester hours of credit are given for two 30-minute lessons per week with practice time being divided almost equally between one and two hours daily. All in all there are as many as 150 variations in the collegiate offering in reference to giving private lessons in music for credit.

TABLE 6

Tabulation and Classification of Private Music Instruction With or Without Credit as Offered in 70 Colleges, Universities, and State Teachers Colleges Out of 541 Responding to Survey

(Showing length and number of lessons, semester hours of credit, and hours of daily practice)

Semester Hours Credit Allowed and Number of Lessons Given per Week		15-Min. Lessons 1 College	25-Min. Lessons 2 Colleges		30-Min. Lessons 56 Colleges							40-Min. Lessons 1 College		45-Min. Lessons 1 College	50-Min. Lessons 5 Colleges				60-Min. Lessons 9 Colleges			
Credit*	Lessons	½	1	2	½	1	1½	2	3	No Req.	No Ind.	2	No Ind.	2	1	1½	2	3	1	1½	2	3
0 hr.	One				2																	
2/5 hr.	One				1																	
1/2 hr.	One					1																
1/2 hr.	Two				1																	
4/5 hr.	Two						1															
2/3 hr.	One			2	2	20				1												
1 hr.	One	1			3	1	1	2			1	1		1	1					2		
1 hr.	Two				2		1															
1 1/3 hr.	One				2			2		1												
1 1/3 hr.	Two				1	1																
1 1/2 hr.	One				1																	
1 1/2 hr.	Two					1																
1 2/3 hr.	One																					
2 hr.	One				3								1						1			
2 hr.	Two			1	7	2	2	12	2								1	1		1		
2 1/2 hr.	Two							2		1									1			
2 2/3 hr.	Two					1		1	1								1					
3 hr.	One						1															
3 hr.	Two					5		2			1						2					
4 hr.	One																				1	
4 hr.	Two				1			4		1										1	1	
5 hr.	Two							3														1
6 hr.	Two					1		2														1

Number of Colleges, with Practice in Clock Hours per Day

80 JUNIOR COLLEGES OUT OF 153 RESPONDING TO SURVEY

(Showing length and number of lessons, semester hours of credit, and hours of daily practice)

Semester Hours Credit Allowed and Number of Lessons Given per Week		25-Min. Lessons 3 Colleges				30-Min. Lessons 65 Colleges						45-Min. Lessons 2 Colleges		50-Min. Lessons 1 College	55-Min. Lessons 1 College		60-Min. Lessons 7 Colleges					
		Number of Colleges, with Practice in Clock Hours per Day																				
Credit*	Lessons	½	1	1½	2	½	1	1½	2	3	4	1	2	1	1	3	1	1½	2	3	4	No. Ind.
1/2 hr.	One						3															
2/3 hr.	One					3		3		1												
1 hr.	One		1			2	27					1					2					
1 hr.	Two	1							2			1										
1 1/3 hr.	One								2													
1 1/3 hr.	Two								2													
1 1/2 hr.	One					2																
1 1/2 hr.	Two						1															
2 hr.	One		2			4		1		3												
2 hr.	Two					6		2	9	1		1			1				2			
2 1/2 hr.	Two							1								1		1				
2 2/3 hr.	Two								2													
3 hr.	One						1															
3 hr.	Two	1			1		2		10	2												
3 hr.	Three						2		2									1				
3 1/2 hr.	Two									1				1								
4 hr.	Two							2		1	1						1					
5 hr.	Two									1												
6 hr.	Three																			1		1

Total number of junior colleges in the United States † 439
Total number of junior colleges that responded to survey (1949–50) 153
Percentage of junior colleges that responded to survey (1949–50) 35

* All credit has been adjusted to semester hour basis. † This total is based on the 1949–50 Educational Directory of the United States Office of Education.

TABLE 8

Tabulation and Classification of Private Music Instruction With or Without Credit as Offered in 15 Junior Colleges Out of 153 Responding to Survey

(Showing length and number of lessons, semester hours of credit, and hours of daily practice)

Semester Hours Credit Allowed and Number of Lessons Given per Week		25-Min. Lessons		30-Min. Lessons						50-Min. Lessons	60-Min. Lessons			
		2 Colleges		10 Colleges						1 College	3 Colleges			
		Number of Colleges, with Practice in Clock Hours per Day												
Credit*	Lessons	1	2	¾	1	1½	2	2½	4	1	1	1½	2	3
0 hr.	One				3									
1 hr.	One	2		1	2					1	1			
2 hr.	One				1		1					1		
2 hr.	Two		1				1	1						
3 hr.	One										1		1	
3 hr.	Two		1			2							1	
4 hr.	Two				1				1					2
6 hr.	Two				1	1								

* All credit has been adjusted to semester hour basis.

Questions and Exercises

1. Why is it likely that the confusion in collegiate music offerings will continue for some time?
2. What should be the goals of the liberal arts college music department?
3. List the obligations of a college music department to its prospective student body.
4. Should the college insist on a high standard of artistic excellence in its musical offerings, or should the music offerings be "socialized"?
5. Should courses in music and art be required of all liberal arts college students?
6. Should all college offerings in music carry credit toward a degree?

Chapter 9

MUSIC TESTS

Educational testing and measuring are as ancient as teaching itself. However, in the modern systematic sense in which these terms are used, they date perhaps only from 1904, when Edward L. Thorndike published his book *An Introduction to the Theory of Mental and Social Measurements*. Thorndike's work ushered in two decades in which testing held a pre-eminent place in the educational thinking of our country. In this period, educational conventions and meetings gave over large portions of their time to intense discussions of problems in measurement. Of course that is not to say that testing and measuring are considered in these more recent years to be of lesser importance, but today they are more generally accepted for what they actually are: implements of authentic education.

Tests are devised to serve many different purposes. Some are designed to diagnose and reveal special weaknesses; some to measure achievement; others to determine aptitude or capacity; and still others to measure ability. In music there have been efforts at devising tests to measure music appreciation. Often many of or all these purposes are attempted in single tests.

The subject of this chapter is tests of musical aptitude. It should be pointed out that, in general, educators regard a pupil's *capability* as a native capacity, organically rooted in the individual. By *musical ability* is meant musical power that has been developed by the individual to greater or lesser degree, depending upon how well he has utilized his capabilities.

CRITERIA FOR MUSICAL TESTS

Determining whether tests for musical aptitude are good or not depends upon several factors: (1) validity; (2) reliability; (3) ease and convenience of administering the tests, and whether the testing procedure required is too expensive to be practicable; (4) whether the devised testing is available to groups of persons or only to individuals; and (5) whether the test findings provide useful information.

Validity. A test is said to be valid if it tests what it sets out to test. To go into a detailed discussion of test validity would involve subjects beyond the purposes of this chapter.[1] Let us imagine a test that is designed to measure ability to sing or play in tune, and that in order to accomplish this end the test is designed to measure power to discriminate between pitches. If, after such a test, those who rated high in the test were, after all, disappointingly unable to learn to sing or play in tune, then it might be concluded that testing for capability in pitch discrimination was not valid for testing an individual's ability to sing or play in tune.[2] Additional testings of other kinds would be indicated.

Reliability. A test is regarded as reliable to the degree that it gives the same results with the same group of students under the same circumstances in repeated testings.

[1] For a technically complete treatment see William A. McCall, *Measurement* (New York: The Macmillan Co., 1939).

[2] Indeed there is sharp difference of opinion as to whether reaction to particular sensory stimuli, such as involved in discriminating between pitches in a nonmusical exercise, has much positive relation to such reaction in a musical situation. See articles by Larson and Mursell in *Third Mental Measurements Yearbook*, pp. 262–64; Carl E. Seashore, *In Search of Beauty in Music* (New York: The Ronald Press Co., 1947), p. 236.

However, unreliability is not always a negative quality inherent in a test.[3] Often a test sets up situations to which the pupils must first learn to adjust before they can respond efficiently. Thus, in addition to repeated testings in order to verify for reliability, the devising of tests of considerable length is wise. However, large portions of a test that are beyond anyone's ability to meet or else within everyone's ability are of little use. Still, each portion of a test should be made up of a sufficiently long list of problems ranging from very easy to very difficult so that the pupils will be "scaled off" as to degrees of aptitude.

Ease, Convenience, and Economy. The requirements for administering a test should not be so complex as to make it impracticable for use. Nor should the test be such that the pupils' success will be dependent to any important degree upon the skill of the administrator. There is also another consideration: While cost does not determine the goodness or badness of a test, it does determine practicability. Tests are of little help if their cost is very high.

Adaptability to Different Situations. This brings us to the question of a test's adaptability to group or school situations. To test pupils individually is all very good but of course very expensive; consequently, schools require tests that can be used in the classroom. Also, while school tests should be long enough to assure reliability, they should be of such kind that they can be given intermittently if need be, or else of such composition that they will not be monotonous or fatiguing. They should lend themselves to being easily transcribed and scored.

[3] It is quite probable that warping in records or changes in line voltage might produce actual pitch variations that differed from the originally recorded tones. Students who heard these would automatically have wrong answers according to the answer key. Such mechanical caprices would break down the reliability of a test depending on high mechanical efficiency.

Usefulness of Information. Of course the test findings should be significant. It is not sufficient that a test give results that are merely interesting in themselves. A test should also provide direction for future teaching. Indeed, the whole philosophy of educational testing is bound up in the teaching imperative of providing guidance for the pupil. This aim should not be forgotten in the casual achievement testing that an instructor employs in his everyday teaching.

Since musical talent is distributed unequally among individuals and since music educators believe that advanced musical accomplishment requires specific talent, many advise that aptitude tests be administered to pupils at the earliest possible time in order to determine their talent.[4] Thus, they believe that the general student and the musical aspirant may be given authentic guidance in order to avoid the unfortunate effects which arise in the personalities of individuals who have not known soon enough about their native capacities. Furthermore, since a serious education in music is extremely expensive, it is hoped that the musical talents of an individual may be determined before his attempts at serious music study prove extravagant.

If dependable musical aptitude tests could be devised, it would be possible to give accurate guidance as to the particular fields in music which the aspirant should enter. For instance, a pupil with a keen sense of pitch discrimination, all other things being equal, would be better suited to playing the violin than one who lacked this sensitive pitch discrimination but who had, perchance, a highly developed motor control which might enable him to study the piano with greater hope for success. Perhaps one of the best reasons for testing musical aptitudes is to provide an incentive for further study. Investigations have shown that many

[4] Many educators feel that the fifth grade is as early as musical testing should be attempted; others feel that the third grade is not too soon.

persons have musical talent who are not aware of it, at least not to the extent of using it very well. Actually, it is observable that only a small percentage of people are definitely unmusical. No doubt many persons could have found a happier lot in life if they had known about and tried to develop their native musical talent.

There are instances in which musical aptitude tests have proved useful for the clinical diagnoses of difficulties, such as in ear or throat defects, that might be improved with physical or medical treatment. Another important value of the aptitude test is seen when children who have begun music study for no reason other than that their parents wish them to learn to play some instrument, are shown, through the tests, to be decidedly unmusical. Authentic aptitude tests will give to the parents of such children a convincing reason for discontinuing expensive special instruction. The teacher also should remember that after finding specific weaknesses in some pupils one must not spend too much extra time with them in hopeless attempts at remedial work, at the expense of the greater needs of the group. But at the same time, the teacher should provide for the child every opportunity to realize with satisfaction whatever potential he does possess, however limited.

Finally, there is value in predicting roughly the degree of attainment which the child might reach. If a pupil gains a high rating on a valid test of rhythmic capability, but falls down in rhythmic performance, the teacher might well investigate to find out whether mental or physical laziness, malnutrition, social maladjustment, or illness is indicated.

CHARACTERISTICS OF TALENT

Many people believe that the talent of an individual is inborn. Experimentation seems to support this view. Children who have not shown certain types of capability and who have been trained intensely over an extended period in the area of their poor capability have regularly shown only small improvement, and even that is probably due to a better understanding of the test and better attention to the problem rather than to improvement of the capability itself. In studying the lives of great musicians, one finds very few who did not manifest talent in their youth. However, it is often difficult to determine whether the child's progress is due to *talent* or *interest*. Many children have been misguided into tragic lives because their *interests* were encouraged beyond what their talents could vocationally satisfy.

Musical talents seem always to develop naturally but sequentially in a routine order of abilities: (1) virtuosity, (2) interpretative power, and (3) creative power. Testing for talent in very young children is hard, first, because of the difficulty of making one's self understood to the child; second, because of the difficulty in making the test intelligible; and third, because of the small child's inability to read.

It is interesting that certain kinds of capability usually connected with musical success deteriorate with age. Musicians have testified that they are positively unable to hear tones that they could hear much earlier in life. Some children with no training can hear higher tones than can some well-trained musicians. It would seem that the *finer* sensibilities in all phases of life tend first to deteriorate as a person grows older. Motor activity also decreases with age.

There is doubt as to whether different phases of talent appear at different ages, that is, whether rhythmic sensitivity develops at one age, pitch discrimination at another, and so on. It would be helpful to know if this were true. The

Vance and Grandprey tests for ranking of nursery school children are interesting in this regard.[5]

Teachers are often asked whether musical talent is dependent upon intelligence. It is not usually possible to answer such a question clearly. Persons of low I.Q. may have a keen capability for discriminating pitch, rhythmic response, and tonal dynamic intensity. On the other hand, abilities in tonal memory and the comprehension of intervals seem to correlate directly with intelligence. There are many difficulties which confront the person attempting to predict or measure musical talent. It is true that one can measure the innate capabilities of a person to perform in certain ways that involve musical experience. Further, one can even measure the ability of the subject as he has established a certain musical power in making use of those capabilities which he has inherited. One can measure, also, something of an individual's achievement in developing detailed acquaintance with the subject of music. But these are only three aspects of a complicated relationship between individuals and music, and it is not possible on the basis of these to evaluate one's musical talent. Of course, without some of the capabilities of which music makes use, one

[5] T. F. Vance and M. B. Grandprey, "Objective Methods of Ranking Nursery School Children on Certain Aspects of Musical Capacity," *Journal of Educational Psychology*, XXII (1931), 577–85.

In this test, measures are taken of (1) responses to music introduced when the children are engaged in other spontaneous interests; (2) responses to the music played during the regular music period when the children receive some encouragement to take part in it; (3) imitations of the nursery school teacher in singing musical intervals. All the foregoing is carried on in group situations; the following measures are carried on privately between the individual child and his teacher: (4) beating time on a triangle to phonograph music; (5) general response to phonograph music; (6) imitating the teacher in beating rhythmical patterns on a triangle; and (7) ratings as based upon musical aspects of the child's home environment.

Among the thirty-one children tested, the highest correlation (0.62±0.13) was found to exist between general responsiveness to music and home background.

would be unlikely to succeed in any serious musical accomplishment; but even so, one should avoid confusing physical sensory capabilities, such as are exercised in musical experiences, with *musical talent*. Although an important part, these are just a part of what is known as musical talent. Since the testing movement is still quite young, especially in music, and not much is known about the authenticity of tests, test results should never be considered as conclusive evidence of musical capability or talent.[6]

It is the author's belief that a person might be described as possessed of great musical talent if he has discriminating sensory capabilities, high general intelligence, a deep interest in and love for music, and a transporting urge to express himself creatively. To regard a person who is lacking in some one of these four essentials as exceptionally talented is perhaps to be unduly optimistic.

[6] In an experiment in 1950, the author tested ninety-seven college students picked at random, using the "Old" Seashore, "New" Seashore, and the Whistler-Thorpe pitch discrimination tests.

Computation of the Pearson Product-Moment coefficients of correlation, checked by the California Test Bureau, revealed these findings:

1. Whistler-Thorpe Pitch Raw Scores vs. New Seashore Pitch Raw Scores 0.506
2. Whistler-Thorpe Pitch Raw Scores vs. Old Seashore Pitch Raw Scores 0.432
3. Whistler-Thorpe Pitch Recognition Raw Scores vs. Whistler-Thorpe Pitch Discrimination Scores 0.264
4. New Seashore Pitch Raw Scores vs. Old Seashore Pitch Raw Scores 0.479

Such low correlation does not seem to justify the confidence in any one of the tests that some vocational counselors feel. Use of any one of the published musical aptitude tests as conclusive basis for advising students about their vocational prospects in music does not seem wise.

Schoen, in his *Psychology of Music*, mentions (p. 184) Seashore's advising that subjects rating in the upper 10 per cent on the Seashore pitch discrimination test be enthusiastically encouraged to study music; in the next 20 per cent, freely encouraged; the next 40 per cent, encouraged; the next 20 per cent, questionably encouraged; the lowest 10 per cent, discouraged. Such advice is temperate. Unfortunately, many counselors use aptitude tests as a sole basis for guiding pupils into or out of music.

Representative Music Tests

Drake Talent Tests

Measure musical capacity of persons of any age, with or without musical training; suggest, however, that eight-year-old children are the youngest that should be tested; test (1) musical memory, (2) interval discrimination, (3) retentivity, and (4) intuition.

These tests are interesting because their content is made up of musical examples. They are economical to give; however, their difficulty makes them unsatisfactory for smaller children. The subjectivity involved because a performer is required to give the test, and the subjective nature of the test on intuition, have caused doubt to arise about the complete adequacies of these measures.

Kwalwasser-Dykema Music Tests

Measure important musical capacities; may be taken by anyone who can understand the directions; norms and a manual of instructions are provided with the records.

These tests consist of ten parts: (1) tonal memory, (2) quality discrimination, (3) intensity discrimination, (4) tonal movement, (5) time discrimination, (6) rhythm discrimination, (7) pitch discrimination, (8) pitch imagery, (9) rhythm imagery, and (10) melodic taste.

In some respects, as in the intensity test where musical tones instead of buzzes or clicks are employed, these tests are superior musically to the older Seashore test; also, the musical quality test of the Kwalwasser-Dykema is an improvement over the consonance test of the old Seashore, because it has a greater correlation with actual music, is only half as long, and yet maintains its effectiveness. Further, this test eliminates to a great degree the possibility of chance. In the tonal memory test of Seashore, the lack of definite tonality would seem to be a musical weakness, although it possesses the highest relationship with music of any of the Seashore tests. The tonal memory tests of both authors, however, measure only momentary musical memory.

The Kwalwasser-Dykema Tonal Movement test may allow for more than one solution depending upon one's taste for progression; so also with the test of melodic taste. It is this subjectivity of setting up esthetic standards that makes the reliability and validity of many of such kinds of tests highly questionable. Since provision for just such subjectivity must be made in any adequate measure of musical talent, the required objectivity in musical talent tests may seem inevitably to destroy the very intrinsic musical values that such tests are actually designed to identify and measure.

Schoen's Tests of Musical Talent

Measure general musicianship of anyone possessed of a reading knowledge of music; require a piano for giving the test; measure (1) absolute pitch and relative pitch, (2) rhythm, and (3) tonal sequence.

These tests are perhaps too difficult for younger children. They are economical to give but are not finely discriminative as measuring implements. The tests are dependent upon the performance and musical ability of the person giving the test. Perhaps tests of additional capabilities such as of time and intensity should be included. The last test (tonal sequence), like the Drake test of intuition, is an effort at measuring esthetic taste, and marks a forward step in attempting to measure musical talent.

Seashore's Measures of Musical Talent

Attempt to measure fundamental musical capacity; serve grades 5–8; norms are furnished for higher grades; consist of six parts: (1) pitch discrimination, (2) intensity discrimination, (3) time discrimination, (4) rhythmic discrimination, (5) consonance discrimination, and (6) tonal memory.

Two series in revised edition of 1940: Series A, designed
for classroom use; Series B, adapted for more exacting work
with special groups and in studios. Test on consonance eliminated; new measure on timbre included.

It can be said of both the Seashore tests that they measure capability, and that musical training does not affect
their results; all the Seashore tests, with the exception of the
consonance test, are objective. There has been, of course,
much variation of opinion as to the reliability and validity
of the Seashore tests. Many educators regard them with
confident approval and some vocational counselors use
them confidently and almost singly as bases for guiding
young people into or out of the field of music. Such trust in
these tests is tragically regrettable. One should not expect
too much from them or from any test. While the new
revised tests furnish a good measure of musical capability,
they hardly provide a complete measure of musical talent
or probable musical accomplishment.

The new Seashore tests are improved recordings. Instead
of the clicks that characterized some of the earliest tests,
the revision employs tonal impulses.

While the author and the revisers of the tests claim great
reliability and validity for them as a measure of musical
capability, it is wise to be reserved in indorsing any tests
that are dependent on phonograph recordings for accuracy.

WHISTLER-THORPE MUSICAL APTITUDE TESTS

Measure musical aptitude in children, 9–15 years of age;
consist of five parts: (1) rhythm recognition, (2) pitch recognition, (3) melody recognition, (4) pitch discrimination,
and (5) advanced rhythm recognition.

Since all the tests are presented by way of the piano, the
effect is realistic and musical, giving the student confidence
that he is meeting real musical problems rather than artificial ones.

Interestingly enough, the authors themselves point out as a strong argument in support of their tests that they rely strictly upon musical examples and that, since hearing differences in pitches of half a vibration per second are not musically realistic, they do not include such problems in their tests. This may be a weakness: it is true that music is not composed to make use of vibration variations of half vibrations per second; nevertheless, a matter of playing on the violin in tune demands that one be able to strike the tone in the center of the appropriate pitch focus. Many would-be violinists are unable to play adequately in tune because they are unable to distinguish when they are missing the tone at, say, a matter of half a vibration or two vibrations per second variation. Of course the objectives of this test are served without requiring fine pitch discrimination.

Questions and Exercises

1. What kinds of music tests are there?
2. Give the factors that mark the quality of a music test.
3. What are the positive values in musical testing? What are the dangers?
4. What are the marks of "musical talent"? List those factors in addition to physical sensibilities that constitute a part of musical talent.
5. Choose two or three well-known tests of musical capability and give them under the best experimental conditions to a large number of persons; under similar conditions do this again a few days later. Compare the results and compute correlation and reliability. Check the results with the tested students' apparent musical success.

APPENDIX

By KARL W. GEHRKENS

This appendix consists of three parts: (a) a terse differentiation in popular language between *philosophy* and *psychology* as these pertain to education; (b) a series of questions concerning the philosophy of music education; (c) a similar series of questions and problems about the psychology of music teaching.

I make no claims of any sort—I am merely trying to get more people to think better about music in human life and music in our schools—which are a part of life.

A. PHILOSOPHY AND PSYCHOLOGY

Philosophy has to do with broad relationships, such as the meaning of life, the function of art, the place of education in the life of men. It deals with such concepts as the good, the true, the beautiful, and its study helps the teacher to decide in what direction he would like to have his pupils go. It makes clearer which things are important and therefore deserving of greater emphasis and which ones are comparatively insignificant. The philosopher tries to see life whole, to understand the relationship of parts to whole. Philosophy should help the teacher to understand the relation of education to life, of any given subject to education as a whole, and of the parts of a subject to the function of the subject in general.

Psychology is the study of human beings and their behavior. It is valuable to the teacher because it shows him how his pupils are likely to react to various stimuli, thus giving him a chance to select and present the particular stimulus that will result in the reaction that he wants from his pupils. In other words, psychology should enable the teacher, at least to a certain extent, to predict and to control the behavior of his pupils—taking behavior in the broad sense, of course.

So philosophy points the way, helps us decide on our general objectives; but psychology shows us how to achieve these objectives in working with our pupils. The conclusion is that both philosophy and psychology are important and that in order to be successful the teacher must be something of a philosopher on the one hand and something of a practical psychologist on the other.

B. MUSIC EDUCATION: SOME PHILOSOPHICAL PROBLEMS

1. In what sense is free universal education the foundation of democracy?

2. How does art, which is a personal, individual experience, affect democracy, which is a group affair?

3. What specific function does the art of music have in a democracy as compared, for example, with poetry, painting, architecture, and other fine arts?

4. What type of school gives the best preparation for citizens who are to participate in a democratic form of government?

5. What place has music in such a school, and how should music study be administered so that it may function in preparing its pupils to participate in the democratic process?

6. How is music to be integrated with other subjects in order to have a maximal effect as an educational subject? (Discuss grades and high school separately.) *Can* music be so integrated and yet not lose its own peculiar place in the educational process?

7. Can music become integrated within itself so as to be of maximum benefit as an educational force; or must we always have jealousy and competition between instrumental and vocal music? Do you think this is an important item and do you expect to take a strong stand, or will you just let things drift and see what happens?

8. Shall music be taught purely as an affair of the feelings; or as dealing mostly with intellectual concepts; or is it possible to combine and integrate the two?

9. Is music being taught in such a way that it helps the school to turn out better individuals who will become better citizens in a democracy? Does it at the same time give experiences in the democratic process itself as a by-product of musical experience?

10. Are school music and community music being closely related so that there is a genuinely integrated musical program in each social unit? Or are school musicians, church musicians, and private teachers indifferent, ignorant concerning, or even hostile in their attitudes toward each other? How do *you* expect to act?

11. Is all this mere theorizing, or is music actually capable of functioning as an important item in the lives of a large number of people?

12. And if music is thus functioning in some community, is it because of school and other influences which are trying to inculcate an appreciation of what is called good music; or is it popular music that is actually contributing the most to wholesome living? Consider the craze for dancing and dance music objectively and try to evaluate in terms of human welfare.

13. If you think good music is failing in its mission, to what do you attribute its failure, and what would you suggest as a remedy? Or are you perfectly satisfied with the results being achieved?

14. If good music is succeeding in some particular community, to what do you attribute its success? (Discuss some fundamental principles and procedures that might be adopted by other communities.)

15. Is music of any real value in time of war? If so, what kind of music? Can you set up some principles or procedures? Or is this, too, just talk?

16. In a financial emergency should music be one of the first things to be eliminated, or one of the last? Be specific in defending your answer.

17. Is music thought of in your own community as a big, important thing, or is it considered to be a frill—a luxury without which one can get along provided he has important things such as food and shelter and safety?

18. Is John Dewey right in his contention that art has been too aristocratic in that it has been regarded as the privilege of a chosen few and isolated to a large extent from the everyday experience of the common people? Is school music in the United States making any contribution to democratizing art, and if so is this contribution actually making a difference in the life of the individual and the well-being of the state? Are we merely building up a system of philosophy and scheme of education which do not really function in human life?

19. If your answer is unfavorable, what can we, the music educators of the present, do about it?

20. Hatred of those who are different from ourselves is one of the greatest obstacles to "Peace on earth, good will to men." Is music capable of making any difference here? Are we teaching our art in such a way that as a by-product of musical skill and appreciation there is developing a greater love of neighbor, a wiser tolerance of differences in race, social station, financial condition, and the like? Or is this none of the music educator's business and is he fulfilling his function if he sees to it that his pupils achieve skill in and appreciation of music?

21. Are music educators as a class by themselves imbued with the real spirit of the artist so that they are able by suggestion and example, as well as through intellectual guidance, to provide children in both grades and high school with genuine esthetic experiences—high moments, moments of exaltation, times when the esthetic glow so permeates their entire being that it actually provides nurture for the spirit? Or is all this merely a theoretical concept consisting mostly of trite and barren formulas which every student of music education must be able to write in his college examination papers or talk about to his school superintendent, but which does not actually function in a practical educational system? Do we music educators ourselves have esthetic thrills, or are we perhaps becoming artisans

rather than artists? And if the latter, then there arises the question: Can an artisan teach an art? Also this one: If music is not taught as an art, is it worth all it costs?

22. Is it possible or desirable to search out, as early as the senior high school level, those pupils who have high musical capacities, all-round intellectual ability, favorable personal traits, and other qualities that would seem to insure success in the field of music education, encouraging such pupils to plan their work and their lives in preparation for the profession of music educator? And should we at the same time discourage those who lack the *combination* of necessary traits from becoming school musicians? Or shall we go on as at present, encouraging anyone who likes music and is good at it to look forward to a musical career, even though we know that the profession is already overcrowded and that success in it is for the comparatively few only? Shall we guide most of our pupils into the world of amateur music, or is the senior high school stage too early for this and must we therefore continue to see thousands, most of whom were predestined to failure, fail in college music courses, or in the field of music education itself?

23. What, finally, do we music educators think of as the really important thing for which we are working? Is it the effect on the individual pupil's spirit of the impact of beauty in the guise of music? Or is it perhaps music's socializing influence on the school as a whole? Or possibly the building of organizations that can win contests and thus bring honor to the school—or to the music director? When the welfare of an organization is at stake, which shall we sacrifice, the individual pupil or the organization? Is Mary assigned to the part for which her voice is adapted, or to the part that needs more singers? Is Johnny encouraged to study the instrument for which he is adapted, or the one that is needed in the band? If the latter, then may we justify our attitude by referring to the greater good of the entire group as compared with what seems to be a smaller good because it pertains to only one pupil? The answers will determine our procedure in thousands of situations and we must think this problem through and decide on some consistent principle.

C. Music Education: Some Psychological Problems

1. The fundamental objective of teaching is to arouse or encourage in the individual a desire to learn. In what respect is music teaching succeeding (or failing) in achieving in pupils the will to learn? Is this the same as *motivation?*

2. "From whole to part" is another command of the psychologist. Are we being consistent in carrying out this principle? (Cite specific instances.)

3. Technical skill is supposed to be acquired as an incidental learning while the pupil is developing musicianship. Is this a feasible approach, or is it necessary to set up technical objectives as ends in themselves? Apply to such items as (1) music reading, and (2) vocal and instrumental technique.

4. How does appreciation develop? Does it come mainly from definitely planned listening lessons; or does it grow naturally as a concomitant of performing ability? Is it a thing that can be set up as an objective or shall we just give the pupil all-round musical experience and hope for the best? Do you appreciate music? If so, where did your appreciation come from? Is your appreciation changing or is it now a fixed thing? What is appreciation; how does a person know whether or not he has it?

5. What effect has the singing experience on the playing of instruments? Is there a definite carry-over or are the two processes entirely different? If the former, name specific items of transfer and suggest methods of bringing about such transfer.

6. Are knowledge of notation and skill in sight singing susceptible of transfer to piano playing, violin playing, etc.? If so, how will you set about devising procedures which will cause the transfer to take place? Is it taking place in the music teaching with which you are familiar? If not, why not?

7. If singing directly affects playing, devise for piano, clarinet, violin, or some other instrument a method which utilizes the possibility of transfer.

8. Is transfer feasible in the elementary phases only, or does it have a place in advanced instruction also? Be specific.

9. If rhythm training is based on large, free bodily movements, as we are told, how is such training to function in the pupil's singing and playing? Or shall we just let the pupil have the fun of the rhythm work and let it go at that? If the former, then devise a method for causing the rhythm that has accumulated from rhythm training to function in playing the piano; the violin; the trumpet.

10. If transfer of rhythm training and sight singing are not taking place in your own teaching, what are you doing about it? Are you just following the methods taught you without really checking and evaluating them in terms of result; or are you being constantly on the alert to see whether your teaching is actually producing the thing that it is supposed to produce?

11. Does this last question make you think harder about what you are supposed to produce and does this lead you to formulate more specific objectives? And is the whole problem now veering toward philosophy, which deals with the *what*, rather than dealing with psychology, which treats of the *how*?

12. The "presence of a group" is supposed to be one of the most powerful incentives for learning; but it can also be a very distracting influence and it can bring about great injustice, especially to very brilliant and very dull pupils. Are we music educators fully aware of both possibilities, and are we planning our work in such a way that group teaching actually becomes an advantage over individual teaching? Is it possible for a teacher to work with a group, and at the same time adapt the activities of the hour to the needs of individual children, thus having each pupil working at appropriate tasks and at the optimum rate for each individual? If this is not feasible, then do we not lose more than we gain? Or does the presence of a group exercise so highly favorable an influence that we gain more than we lose even though the system is admittedly imperfect?

NOTE: The above list is by no means complete and you might well think through and formulate in good English additional problems. Then you should formulate a series of tersely expressed *principles* on the basis of which you expect to devise your own methods and procedures.

BIBLIOGRAPHY

I. REFERENCES ARRANGED BY CHAPTER

CHAPTER 1

THE HISTORY OF MUSIC EDUCATION IN THE UNITED STATES

American History and Encyclopedia of Music. Toledo: I. Squire, 1908–10.
In its time this 12-volume collection, edited by W. L. Hubbard, was very useful for the musical layman; the volume on American music is good.

BIRGE, EDWARD B. *History of Public School Music in the United States.* Philadelphia: Oliver Ditson Co., 1939.
A mine of information concerning the development of public school music.

ELSON, LOUIS C. *The History of American Music.* New York: The Macmillan Co., 1925.
This excellent volume is one of the first to attempt a complete compilation of the growth of musical institutions in the United States.

EWEN, DAVID. *Music Comes to America.* New York: Allen, Towne & Heath, Inc., 1947.
Palatably written, this book introduces the reader to the several musical categories of activity in the United States which indicate arrival at maturity; has an interesting chapter on horizons for music education.

"Fifty Years of Music Education in America," *Music Educators Journal.* (April–May, June–July, 1950).
A review of music education in first half of 20th century by Frances Elliott Clark; Edward Bailey Birge; Edgar B. Gordon; Herman F. Smith; and Lilla Belle Pitts.

FINKELSTEIN, SIDNEY. *Jazz.* New York: The Citadel Press, 1948.
A faithful, authentic, though unorthodox appraisal of jazz; provides important information for the musician and the novice.

FORD, IRA W. *Traditional Music of America.* New York: Thomas Y. Crowell Co., 1936.
This invaluable book interestingly recounts the story of three hundred years of American music history.

International Cyclopedia of Music and Musicians, 4th ed. New York: Dodd, Mead & Co., Inc., 1946.
Oscar Thompson, formerly editor-in-chief, now deceased, is succeeded by Nicolas Slonimsky, editor of this fourth edition; carrying

out the policy evidenced in each of the earlier editions, the new volume is an improved, extended, more scholarly work.

KAUFFMAN, HARRY M. *A History of the Music Educators National Conference.* Nashville: George Peabody College for Teachers, 1942.
A Doctor of Philosophy dissertation.

MACDOUGALL, HAMILTON C. *Early New England Psalmody.* Brattleboro, Vt.: Stephen Daye Press, 1940.
Detailed information about and analyses of the religious music of early New England.

CHAPTER 2

A PHILOSOPHY OF MUSIC EDUCATION

BENSON, BARBARA E. *Music and Sound Systems in Industry.* New York: McGraw-Hill Book Co., Inc., 1945.
The first book treating industrial uses of music; tells how to direct, build, and broadcast musical programs throughout an industrial plant.

COLEMAN, SATIS NARRONA. *Creative Music in the Home.* Valparaiso, Ind.: L. E. Myers & Co., 1927.
Tells how to make simple musical instruments out of household articles; includes numerous tunes using number notation so that the small child may read and play the music.

DICKINSON, EDWARD. *The Education of a Music Lover.* New York: Charles Scribner's Sons, 1911.
This profound book presents material that is indispensable to the serious listener; music educators who are familiar with its contents recognize its importance.

FARNSWORTH, CHARLES H. *Education Through Music.* New York: American Book Co., 1909.
The oldest book dealing specifically and broadly with music as an educational subject; it is still pertinent and important.

FARNSWORTH, P. R. *Musical Taste: Its Measurement and Cultural Nature.* See listing under Chapter 9.

GREENE, THEODORE M. *The Arts and the Art of Criticism.* Princeton: Princeton University Press, 1940.
This volume endeavors to investigate the unexplored no man's land lying between art and philosophy; it is an important, serious work. See dissertation, Squire, Russel N. *The Philosophy of Music of George Santayana, Helen Huss Parkhurst, and Theodore Meyer Greene.* New York: New York University, 1942.

JOHNSON, HARRIET. *Your Career in Music.* New York: E. P. Dutton & Co., Inc., 1946.
Provides definite, authentic, vocational information about music; does not indulge in sugar-coating.

LICHT, SIDNEY. *Music in Medicine.* Boston: New England Conservatory of Music, 1946.

A physician provides objective counsel about the use of music as an aid in therapy.

McKinney, Howard D. *Music and Man*. New York: American Book Co., 1948.
A sociological approach to the development of understanding of music; surveys contemporary United States music; indicates musical beginnings and touches upon structural principles in musical composition.

Mursell, James L. *Human Values in Music Education*. New York: Silver Burdett Co., 1934.
An effective introduction to a philosophy of music education.

Neumeyer, Martin H., and Neumeyer, Esther S. *Leisure and Recreation*. New York: A. S. Barnes & Co., 1949.
Studies leisure and recreation in their sociological reference, providing material on social group work and information on research in the field.

Schullian, Dorothy M., and Schoen, Max. *Music and Medicine*. New York: Henry Schuman, Inc., 1948.
Examines music as a therapeutic; is a series of essays by eminent students and authorities in the several phases of the subject.

Seashore, Carl E. *In Search of Beauty in Music*. New York: The Ronald Press Co., 1947.
Presents a scientific approach to musical esthetics; is a compilation of previously published articles on the psychology of music as investigated at the University of Iowa.

Soibelman, Doris. *Therapeutic and Industrial Uses of Music*. New York: Columbia University Press, 1948.
An objective survey of the problems involved in functional applications of music; reports on and appraises some of the experiments and findings; provides an excellent bibliography.

Van de Wall, Willem. *Music in Institutions*. New York: Russell Sage Foundation, 1936.
The author writes authentically and sympathetically in the area of music as an aid in psychiatry.

Chapter 3

EDUCATIONAL CONTINUITY AT DIFFERENT LEVELS

Davison, Archibald T. *Music Education in America*. New York: Harper & Bros., 1926.
Appraises critically the pedagogy of current music education; much of the opinion in it is justifiable and helpful although frequently it evidences a lack of contact with mass musical education of children in the grass roots regions of the country.

Mursell, James L. *Music in American Schools*. New York: Silver Burdett Co., 1943.

An important book restating and extending views which have identified the author as a leader in music educational thought.

PERHAM, BEATRICE. *Music in the New School*. Chicago: Neil A. Kjos
Music Co., 1941.
Explains in stimulating fashion the viewpoint of the progressive
educator.

PITTS, LILLA BELLE. *The Music Curriculum in a Changing World*. New
York: Silver Burdett Co., 1944.
Vividly and excitingly presents the concept of learning through
music in order to live a full, rich life as an integrated personality;
gives the music educator a base upon which to meet the general
educator.

CHAPTER 4

MUSIC IN THE ELEMENTARY SCHOOL

BARBOUR, HARRIET BUXTON, and FREEMAN, W. S. *Children's Record
Book*. New York: Oliver Durrell, Inc., 1947.
An authoritative guide to excellent recorded music for children from
six months to sixteen years.

BROOKS, MARIAN B., and BROWN, HARRY A. *Music Education in the Elementary School*. New York: American Book Co., 1946.
Serves well as a textbook in teacher-training institutions; is dynami-
cally modern; best used under the guidance of a mature teacher.

BURCH, GLADYS. *Modern Composers for Boys and Girls*. New York: A. S.
Barnes & Co., 1941.
Contains biographical sketches of twenty composers; prepared to
meet the interest of boys and girls.

CHRISTIANSON, HELEN MARGUERITE. *Music and the Young Child*. Washington, D.C.: Association for Childhood Education, 1936.
Tells the role of music in the life of the small child; suggests methodology in pre-school and kindergarten; includes essays by Alice
Thorn and Beatrice Perham.

COLEMAN, SATIS NARRONA. *Creative Music for Children*. New York:
G. P. Putnam's Sons, 1922.
Suggests a plan for calling from the children a natural development
in music; tells how to make instruments; suggests applications in
poetry, dancing, singing.

CONNETTE, EARLE. "Bibliography in Music Education for Classroom
Teachers," *Elementary School Journal*, December, 1938.
An article providing a practical bibliography to meet the everyday
detail problems in music which confront the general teacher.

FOX, LILLIAN MOHR, and HOPKINS, L. T. *Creative School Music*. New
York: Silver Burdett Co., 1936.
Provides practical information for the teacher and the supervisor in
the elementary school, in reference to fostering children's extended
interests in creativity.

GEHRKENS, KARL W. *Introduction to School Music Teaching.* Boston: C. C. Birchard & Co., 1919.
    Although published over thirty years ago, this book raised problems and questions about elementary and secondary school music that still need to be answered today.

————. *Music in the Grade Schools.* Boston: C. C. Birchard & Co., 1934.
    For years this was the most complete book on elementary school music education; it is authoritative, still pertinent and important.

GRANT, PARKS. *Music for Elementary Teachers.* New York: Appleton-Century-Crofts, Inc., 1951.
    Designed to actually teach the music itself to the prospective general elementary school teacher who at the same time studies methods and materials of elementary school music education.

JACQUES-DALCROZE, EMILE. *Rhythm, Music and Education.* New York: G. P. Putnam's Sons, 1931.
    Presents an authoritative system of rhythm training.

JERSILD, A. T., and BEINSTOCK, L. *Development of Rhythm in Young Children.* (Child Development Monograph.) New York: Teachers College, 1935.
    A psychologist and an educator discuss the psychology of the child as evidenced in sensitivity to rhythm.

McCONATHY, OSBOURNE, et al. *Music in Rural Education.* New York: Silver Burdett Co., 1923.
    Provides a program of music for the one- and two-room school; is based on the "Music Hour" music series published by Silver Burdett Company.

Music Education in the Elementary School. Sacramento: California State Department of Education, 1944.
    Outlines a state course of study, providing careful analyses and suggestions for many different categories of the subject; edited by leaders in western music education: Helen Heffernan, Mary E. Ireland, and others.

MUSIC EDUCATION RESEARCH COUNCIL. *Course of Study in Music for Rural Schools.* Chicago: Music Educators National Conference. Bulletin No. 19, 1936.
    Presents a detailed schedule of offerings with a clear statement of objectives and philosophy in rural music education.

Music Education Source Book. Chicago: Music Educators National Conference, 1947.
    Includes bibliography; listings of materials, recordings, scores, research findings in the whole field of music education; represents the work of hundreds of contributors; edited by Hazel Nohavec Morgan.

MYERS, LOUISE KIFER. *Teaching Children Music in the Elementary School.* New York: Prentice-Hall, Inc., 1950.
    A guide as to music method, materials, and philosophy for the general teacher in the "new school."

National Elementary Principal. Washington, D. C.: National Education Association (February, 1951).

> Contains a list of books about music, musicians, and instruments for elementary schools; devotes its entire contents to music education.

NEWMAN, ELIZABETH. *Music for Teeny and Tiny.* New York: Creative Music Publishers, 1942.

> Plans a course of musical experience for pre-school children, to be used by mothers and teachers; is suitable for use with individual children or groups of children.

PERKINS, CLELLA LESTER. *How to Teach Music to Children.* Chicago: Hall & McCreary Co., 1936.

> In addition to a discussion of teaching techniques, includes a considerable number of songs, some with piano accompaniments.

RCA Victor Record Library for Elementary Schools. 85 records. Grades 1–3; 4–6.

SHAFER, MARY SHERMAN. *Rhythm for Children.* New York: A. S. Barnes & Co., 1938.

> Contains games and material for musico-calisthenics.

STINSON, ETHELYN LENORE. *How to Teach Children Music.* New York: Harper & Bros., 1941.

> Reports on how to teach music to mentally retarded or to otherwise handicapped children; title is misleading.

CHAPTER 5

MUSIC IN THE JUNIOR HIGH SCHOOL

BATES, JAMES. *Voice Culture for Children.* New York: H. W. Gray Co., 1907.

> This early study is still important and helpful.

BEATTIE, JOHN W., McCONATHY, OSBOURNE, and MORGAN, RUSSELL, V. *Music in the Junior High School.* New York: Silver Burdett Co., 1930.

> An important book discussing music in the junior high school from a broad educational viewpoint.

DAWSON, JOHN T. *The Voice of the Boy.* New York: Laidlaw Bros., 1919.

> Studies the nature and needs of the boy's voice and compares it with the adult's voice.

GEHRKENS, KARL W. *Music in the Junior High School.* Boston: C. C. Birchard & Co., 1936.

> This very complete treatment is intended for both the teacher and the prospective teacher; it is based upon fundamental principles of psychology and philosophy.

McCONATHY, OSBOURNE, *et al. Music in Rural Education.* See listing under Chapter 4.

MUSIC EDUCATION RESEARCH COUNCIL. *Course of Study in Music for Rural Schools.* See listing under Chapter 4.

Music Education Source Book. See listing under Chapter 4.

NORMANN, THEODORE. *Instrumental Music in the Public Schools.* Philadelphia: Oliver Ditson Co., 1941.
    Discusses class methods of teaching instruments; contains chapters on both elementary and high school instrumental music.

PITTS, CAROL. *Pitts Voice Class Method.* Chicago: Neil A. Kjos Music Co., 1936.
    Contains elementary exercises and simple songs for one, two, three, or four voices with suggestions for improving tone and breathing.

PITTS, LILLA BELLE. *Music Integration in the Junior High School.* Boston: C. C. Birchard & Co., 1936.
    The author, an experienced teacher, emphasizes the correlating of music with other school activities; she suggests well-planned procedures for educating the pupil through music.

CHAPTER 6

MUSIC IN THE SENIOR HIGH SCHOOL

BEER, A. S. "Music and the Exceptional Child," *Music Educators Journal* (November, 1950), 46, 47.
    Voices a plea for workers in serving needs of exceptional children, mentally dull, physically handicapped; tells of success of actual projects in the Ann J. Kellogg School, Battle Creek, Michigan.

DYKEMA, PETER, and GEHRKENS, KARL W. *The Teaching and Administration of High School Music.* Boston: C. C. Birchard & Co., 1941.
    Covers all phases of music teaching in the high school: vocal, instrumental, theoretical, administrative; suggests materials and equipment; contains over 600 pages and 150 illustrations.

GEHRKENS, KARL W. *Introduction to School Music Teaching.* See listing under Chapter 4.

GILLILAND, ESTHER GOETZ. "Prescriptions Set to Music," *Exceptional Children* (December, 1951), 68–70.
    Reports on the benefits for the physically handicapped of using instruments of proper sorts to strengthen muscles and improve coordination.

McCONATHY, OSBOURNE, et al. *Music in Rural Education.* See listing under Chapter 4.

MUSIC EDUCATION RESEARCH COUNCIL. *Course of Study in Music for Rural Schools.* See listing under Chapter 4.

Music Education Source Book. See listing under Chapter 4.

NORMANN, THEODORE. *Instrumental Music in the Public Schools.* See listing under Chapter 5.

PIERCE, ANNE, and LIEBLING, ESTELLE. *Class Lessons in Singing.* New York: Silver Burdett Co., 1937.
    Suitable for senior high and college students; contains songs and excerpts and lists of other songs.

PITTS, CAROL. *Pitts Voice Class Method.* See listing under Chapter 5.

WARD, ARTHUR E. *Music Education for High Schools.* New York: American Book Co., 1941.
> Enthusiastically exhorts the teacher to develop the native and profound interests that high school pupils have for music; treats the field comprehensively.

WILSON, HARRY R. *Music in the High School.* New York: Silver Burdett Co., 1941.
> Attempts to tell the why of music education in order to determine the what and the how; the book is important.

CHAPTER 7

SOME NEEDS FOR PUBLIC MUSIC EDUCATION TODAY

BANSE, A. M. "Whither Music Supervision in the Elementary School?" *Music Educators Journal,* September, 1949, pp. 48, 50.
> Decries the trend toward eliminating supervision of the general elementary school teaching of music.

CLARKE, E. T. "Can Music Teachers Be Artists and Educators?" Music Teachers National Association *Procedures,* 1939.
> Reports on the Association of American Colleges project under which music teachers who are also performing artists are enabled to tour on short leave from their own colleges in order to perform on other campuses bringing to them unique programs of significant music.

CONNETTE, E. "Administrative Criticism of Music Teaching." *Journal of Educational Research,* December, 1942, pp. 254–68.
> A report on a survey of 879 school administrators as to needs in the training of prospective music teachers.

Gifted Children. Edited by Pane Witty for American Association for Gifted Children. Boston: D. C. Heath & Co., 1951.
> Guidance for working with gifted children; refers somewhat to use of music. Does this indicate that music educators need to explore the field more completely?

McCOWEN, E. R. "Administrator's Point of View," *Educational Music Magazine,* March, 1947, pp. 18–19, 58–59.
> A county superintendent outlines and defends a complete vocal and instrumental music program from grade one through grade twelve.

MUSIC EDUCATION RESEARCH COUNCIL. "Music Supervision and Administration in the Schools." Chicago: Music Educators National Conference, 1949.
> A report on history, present status, and objectives of music supervision, prepared by C. M. Dennis, P. Dykema, and others.

"Needs, Opportunities, Plans and Prospects," *Music Educators Journal,* June, 1946, pp. 14–17.
> A symposium to which Helen M. Hosmer, Lloyd V. Funchess, Lorin F. Wheelwright, Hugh E. McMillen, Marguerite V. Hood, and

Stanley M. Teel contributed; presents concisely specific suggestions under the topics (1) Music for Abundant Living, (2) For World Fellowship, (3) A Happier Way, (4) For More Effective Teaching, (5) Our Musical Resources, and (6) We Must Still Plan Ahead.

NICKERSON, J. F. "An Inventory of Audio-Visual Aids," *Educational Music Magazine* (September, 1950), 21, 52–56.

Warns that seeming inadequacy of newer devices in "audio-visual" education is often result of using such devices when less novel devices are still more effective; advocates more experimenting; using of newer devices when they can do a job others cannot do.

SHEEHY, E. D. "Music and the Classroom Teacher," *Music Educators Journal,* September, 1950, pp. 36–37.

Taking for granted the need for music supervision of the general teacher, suggests the setting up of music workshops for providing in-service musical training; recounts the experiences of one successful classroom program.

SOMMERS, H. H. "Responsibility of Music Education," *Music Educators Journal,* June, 1947, pp. 16–17, 58–59.

A high school principal points out that music in the schools must help in the attainment of peace and security through "quickening of American spirit, a deepening of emotion and sentiment, and a mounting sense of seriousness and integrity" and regard for the inalienable human rights.

CHAPTER 8

MUSIC IN THE COLLEGE

JEFFERS, EDMUND V. *Music for the General College Student.* New York: King's Crown Press, 1944.

Advocates providing music for the liberal arts student so that he may enjoy music in his non-professional life.

JONES, VINCENT. *Music Education in the College.* Boston: C. C. Birchard & Co., 1949.

Treats in considerable detail the status of music in the college, the philosophy supporting its inclusion, and some of the practical processes in making its place in the college significant.

Music Education Source Book. See listing under Chapter 4.

Music in the Liberal Arts College. Oberlin: Music Teachers National Association, 1935.

Presents papers read on subjects of curriculum, awarding of credit, meeting needs of general student.

MUSIC TEACHERS NATIONAL ASSOCIATION. *Papers and Proceedings.* Published annually since 1906.

Contain valuable materials and records; useful to the teacher of music, whether in private instruction or in school work.

NATIONAL ASSOCIATION OF SCHOOLS OF MUSIC. *A Musical Literature List for Music School Libraries*. Published by the Association from time to time.

THOMPSON, RANDALL. *College Music*. New York: The Macmillan Co., 1935.
Reports on a survey of thirty representative colleges as to music curriculums and philosophies.

CHAPTER 9

MUSIC TESTS

BROOKS, B. MARIAN, and BROWN, HARRY A. *Music Education in the Elementary School*. See listing under Chapter 4.

BUCHANAN, WALTER. "The Nature of Rhythmic Talent," *The Pacific Spectator* (Summer, 1951), 342–347.
Analyzes rhythmic abilities, indicates that rhythmic power is learned; reports on characteristics of singers and instrumentalists and upon apparent differences among races and cultures.

CHANDLER, ALBERT R., and BARNHART, EDWARD N. *A Bibliography of Psychological and Experimental Aesthetics*. Berkeley: University of California Press, 1938.
A comprehensive bibliography of importance to serious students in the field.

FARNSWORTH, PAUL R. *Musical Taste: Its Measurement and Cultural Nature*. Stanford: Stanford University Press, 1950.
Describes musical taste on the basis of findings from a poll of listeners; is a psychology of human interest in music; suggests that musical taste is a "phenomenon of the social sciences," music is not good or bad in terms of inherent qualities.

GAW, E. A. "A Revision of the Consonance Test," *Psychological Monographs*, XXV, No. 2 (1918), 134–47.
A report on Malmberg's study of consonance in which a revision eliminating undesirable intervals and simplifying the description of consonance is set forth; a preliminary norm for children is also established.

GEHRKENS, KARL W. *Music in the Grade Schools*. See listing under Chapter 4.

GILDERSLEEVE, GLENN. "Standards and the Evaluation and Measurement of Achievement in Music," *Music Education, Thirty-fifth Yearbook of the National Society for the Study of Education*. Bloomington, Ind.: Public School Publishing Co., 1936.
Examines the common criteria for measuring achievement: (1) performance, (2) liking for music as an achievement in appreciation and assimilation, (3) preference for certain kinds of music, and (4) preference for certain kinds of music production, radio, phonograph, or concert.

HILDRETH, GERTRUDE H. *A Bibliography of Mental Tests and Rating Scales*. New York: The Psychological Corp., 1939.
  The recognized bibliographical compilation in reference to psychological test and measurement.

KWALWASSER, JACOB. *Tests and Measurements in Music*. Boston: C. C. Birchard & Co., 1927.
  Up to its time, the only book offering material on musical tests.

LOWERY, H. "Musical Memory," *British Journal of Psychology*, XIX (1928–29), 397–404.
  A review of the problems connected with testing for musical memory, and a report on the results of such a test showing correlation between musical memory and intelligence.

————. "Cadence and Phrase Tests in Music," *British Journal of Psychology*, XVII (1926), 111–18.
  Describes the nature of cadence and phrase tests, setting forth the results of preliminary testing in concise tables.

MAINWARING, JAMES. "Experiments on the Analysis of Cognitive Processes Involved in Musical Ability and in Musical Education," *British Journal of Educational Psychology*, I (1931), 180–203.
  An analysis of the cognitive processes involved in musical ability as evidenced in response to pitch intensity and duration; studies phenomena such as the musical emphases that are attained through highness of pitch, or loudness of tone; investigates how combinations of these suggest effects different from the actual nature of the musical stimulus.

————. "Kinaesthetic Factors in the Recall of Musical Experience," *British Journal of Psychology*, XXIII (1932–33), 284–307.
  An investigation involving the introspection of children and adults who answer questions about music they have previously listened to; suggests that some kind of kinaesthetic behavior is essential to adequate musical memory.

MALMBERG, C. F. "The Perception of Consonance and Dissonance," *Psychological Monographs*, XXV, No. 2 (1918), 93–113.
  An attempt (1) to describe the nature of consonance, (2) to identify its elements, and (3) to rank musical intervals within the octave c'–c" in the order of degree of consonance.

MURSELL, JAMES L., and GLENN, MABELLE. *Psychology of School Music Teaching*. New York: Silver Burdett Co., 1938.
  Investigates in a stimulating manner the psychological processes of teaching; contains an interesting description of many of the important music tests.

SCHOEN, MAX. "Bibliography of Experimental Studies in the Psychology of Music," Music Teachers National Association *Proceedings*, 1940, 41, 42.
  A very complete listing extended through the succeeding years.

————. *The Psychology of Music*. New York: The Ronald Press Co., 1940.

A comprehensive bibliography and report on findings in the field to date.

SCHOEN, MAX. *The Understanding of Music.* New York: Harper & Bros., 1945.
    Attempts to tell how to cultivate the musically aesthetic response; although occasionally abstruse, is important and challenging, especially to the general music lover or critic.

SEASHORE, CARL E. *The Psychology of Music.* New York: McGraw-Hill Book Co., Inc., 1939.
    An important report on the findings in music testing as carried on by the author, and a realistic study of the psychology of music.

————. *In Search of Beauty in Music.* See listing under Chapter 2.

Third Mental Measurements Yearbook. New Brunswick: Rutgers University Press, 1949.
    Edited by Oscar K. Buros, this is the authoritative reference work in the field.

VANCE, T. F., and GRANDPREY, M. B. "Objective Methods of Ranking Nursery School Children on Certain Aspects of Musical Capacity," *Journal of Educational Psychology,* XXII, 577–85.
    Measures nursery school children's responses to music in both classroom situations and private interviews with the teacher.

Achievement Tests in Music

ALLEN, RICHARD D., BUTTERFIELD, WALTER, and TULLY, MARGUERITE. *Providence Inventory Test in Music.* New York: World Book Co., 1932.

GILDERSLEEVE, GLENN. *Music-Achievement Tests.* New York: Bureau of Publications, Teachers College, Columbia University, 1922.

HILLBRAND, E. K. *Sight-Singing Test.* New York: World Book Co., 1923.

KELSEY, JULIA T. *Kelsey Standardized Tests of Musical Achievement.* Cincinnati: C. A. Gregory Co., 1931.

MADISON, THURBER HULL. *Interval Discrimination as a Measure of Musical Aptitude.* New York: Columbia University Archives of Psychology, 1942.

MOSHER, R. M. *A Study of the Group Method of Measurement of Sight-Singing.* New York: Bureau of Publications, Teachers College, Columbia University, 1925.

Aptitude Tests in Music

DRAKE, R. M. *Tests of Musical Talent.* Bloomington, Ind.: Public School Publishing Co., 1934. See discussion, Chapter 9, p. 139.

KWALWASSER, JACOB. *Kwalwasser Tests of Melodic and Harmonic Sensitivity.* Camden: Victor Talking Machine Co., 1926.

KWALWASSER, JACOB, and DYKEMA, PETER. *Kwalwasser-Dykema Musical Talent Tests.* Chicago: Carl Fischer Co., 1930. See discussion, Chapter 9, p. 139.

KWALWASSER, JACOB, and RUCH, G. M. *Test of Musical Accomplishment.* Iowa City: Bureau of Educational Research and Service, State University of Iowa, 1924.

MAINWARING, JAMES. "Test of Musical Ability," *British Journal of Educational Psychology,* I (1931), 313–21.

RÉVÉCZ, GEZA. "Prüfung der Musikalität," *Zeitschrift für Psychologie,* LXXXV (1920), 163–209.

RUPP, HANS. "Ueber die Prüfung Musikalischer Fähigkeiten, Teil I," *Zeitschrift für Angewandte Psychologie,* 1915, Vol. IX, 1–76.

SAETVEIT, JOSEPH G., et al. *Revision of the Seashore Measures of Musical Talent.* Iowa City: University of Iowa Press, 1940.

SCHOEN, MAX. "Tests of Musical Feeling and Understanding," in *The Psychology of Music.* New York: The Ronald Press Co., 1940, pp. 175–77. See discussion, Chapter 9, p. 140.

SEASHORE, C. E. *Measures of Musical Talent.* Rev.; Camden: Victor Talking Machine Co., 1940. See discussion, Chapter 9, p. 140.

SEREJSKI, M., and MALTZEN, C. VON. "Prüfung der Musikalität nach der Testmethode," *Psychotechnische Zeitschrift,* III (1928), 103–7.

WHISTLER, HARVEY S., and THORPE, LOUIS P. *Tests of Musical Aptitude.* Los Angeles: California Test Bureau, 1950. See discussion, Chapter 9, p. 141.

II. ADDITIONAL REFERENCES

ACTIVITIES IN MUSIC

ABBOTT, GEORGE J. *Instrumental Music in the Public Schools.* Boston: C. C. Birchard & Co., 1935.

   Suitable as a reference book; lists typical problems with solutions given by an experienced instrumental teacher.

BALLIETT, MELVIN L. *Music Library Manual.* Elkhart, Ind.: H. & A. Selmer, Inc., 1940.

   Gives detailed instructions for cataloguing, filing, and distributing music organizations materials.

BRAND, ERICK D. *Selmer Band Instrument Repairing Manual.* Elkhart, Ind.: H. & A. Selmer, Inc., 1942.

   Provides complete and authentic guidance in instrument repair.

CHRISTY, VAN A. *Glee Club and Chorus.* New York: G. Schirmer, Inc., 1940.

   Deals with organizing and conducting choral groups; suggests materials; especially helpful to the beginning conductor.

DVORAK, RAYMOND. *The Band on Parade.* New York: Carl Fischer, Inc., 1937.

   Provides practical and useful information on marching, maneuvering, baton twirling.

GALLO, STANISLAO. *The Modern Band.* Boston: C. C. Birchard & Co., 1939, Vols. I and II.
>Replete with excellent score examples; provides scholarly material about instruments and instrumentation.

GOLDMAN, RICHARD FRANKO. *The Band's Music.* New York: Pitman Publishing Co., 1938.
>Includes historical information about wind instruments, and provides lists of original and arranged works for band.

———. *The Concert Band.* New York: Rinehart & Co., Inc., 1946.
>Discusses instrumentation of respective bands, upon which the kind of music chosen for them is dependent; challenges band educators by showing that present-day high school bands determine the future quality of band music.

HINDSLEY, MARK H. *School Band and Orchestra Administration.* New York: Boosey & Hawkes, Inc., 1948.
>Serves the needs of the expert instrumental music educator who needs to learn more about administration and school procedures.

McCONATHY, OSBOURNE, MORGAN, RUSSELL V., and CLARK, HARRY L. *School and Community Band and Orchestra Series with Manual.* Boston: Oliver Ditson Co., 1928.
>Includes principles of pedagogy and provides ample materials.

NEWTON, LEONARD G., and YOUNG, T. CAMPBELL. *The Book of the School Orchestra.* New York: Carl Fischer, Inc., 1936.
>Contains list of suitably graded music and discussion of methodology.

ZANZIG, AUGUSTUS D. *Starting and Maintaining a Community Orchestra.* New York: National Recreation Association, 1940.
>Gives guidance in developing neighborhood orchestral activity centered in the school.

APPRECIATION OF MUSIC

BALDWIN, LILLIAN L. *Introduction to Chamber Music for Listeners.* Cleveland: Severance Hall, 1945.
>This is a specially prepared publication that was released a few years ago for distribution at Severance Hall, home of the Cleveland Orchestra. Provides delightful notes on and descriptions of chamber music especially useful for perusal as one listens to the music.

———. *A Listener's Anthology of Music.* New York: Silver Burdett C 1948.
>An important work in two volumes. Presents the significant and representative ages in music with a discussion of the composers' works.

BARTON, FREDERICK BUSHNELL. *Music as a Hobby.* New York: Harper & Bros., 1941.
>Tells in the most practical fashion how to have fun with music; even tells how to get your son interested in music.

EARHART, WILL. *The Meaning and Teaching of Music*. New York: Witmark & Sons, 1935.
> Presents to the serious student a broad vision of the meaning of music in life.

FARNSWORTH, PAUL R. *Musical Taste: Its Measurement and Cultural Nature*. Stanford: Stanford University Press, 1950. See listing under Chapter 9.

FOX, LILLIAN MOHR, and HOPKINS, L. T. *Creative School Music*. See listing under Chapter 4.

GEHRKENS, KARL W. *The Fundamentals of Music*. Boston: Oliver Ditson Co., 1924.
> This famous book serves as a reference work for college students enrolled in music education and appreciation courses; is a good survey for music teachers already in the field, whether associated with public, parochial, or private school.

HAGGIN, B. H. *A Book of the Symphony*. New York: Oxford University Press, 1937.
> Analyzes the best-known works of Haydn, Mozart, Beethoven, Schubert, Brahms, Tchaikovsky, and Franck in a way peculiarly adaptable to phonograph listening; attempts to make musical meaning clear to the untrained listener.

———. *Music on Records*. New York: Alfred A. Knopf, Inc., 1941.
> Provides an authentic although iconoclastic criticism of recorded music; valuable for the serious listener.

JONES, VINCENT, and BAILEY, BERTHA WINGATE. *Exploring Music*. Boston: C. C. Birchard & Co., 1941.
> Guides the student of high school or junior college into heartening experiences with music that will enable him to increase his appreciation.

McKINNEY, HOWARD D., and ANDERSON, W. R. *Discovering Music*. New York: American Book Co., 1934.
> Guides the musical novitiate toward enjoyment, understanding, and appreciation of music, using for examples phonographically recorded music.

MOORE, DOUGLAS S. *Listening to Music*. New York: W. W. Norton & Co., Inc., 1937.
> A book on music appreciation; provides analyses and interpretations of music.

OBERNDORFER, ANNE SHAW. *What We Hear in Music*. Camden, N. J.: RCA Manufacturing Co., Inc. (Education Department), 1936.
> Provides a complete, thorough, and authoritative compendium of information for the development of music appreciation.

STRINGHAM, EDWIN J. *Listening to Music Creatively*. New York: Prentice-Hall, Inc., 1946.
> Adequate as a classroom text, but is not as satisfactory for individual use; makes good use of reference to recordings; emphasizes romantic and later periods.

WELCH, ROY D. *The Appreciation of Music.* New York: Harper & Bros., 1945.
> Provides tasks which, upon completion, will help the reader to develop his appreciation of music.

CONDUCTING

BAKALEINIKOFF, VLADIMIR. *Elementary Rules of Conducting.* New York: Boosey, Hawkes, Belwin, Inc., 1938.
> A useful, practical manual for the high school conductor of band or orchestra.

DAVISON, ARCHIBALD. *Choral Conducting.* Cambridge: Harvard University Press, 1940.
> Includes valuable aids; written by one of the most distinguished choral directors in the United States.

EARHART, WILL. *Choral Technics.* New York: Witmark & Sons, 1937.
> A national authority in music education suggests technics of great value; should be used with the manual, published in 1938, which includes important lists of materials.

EWEN, DAVID. *The Man with the Baton.* New York: Thomas Y. Crowell Co., 1936.
> Inspiringly reviews the work of a long line of great and musicianly conductors; useful not only to the teacher of instrumental music, but to the general music lover as well.

FINN, WILLIAM J. *The Art of the Choral Conductor.* Boston: C. C. Birchard & Co., 1939.
> This extremely important book should be studied by both amateur and professional choral conductors.

GEHRKENS, KARL W. *Essentials in Conducting.* Boston: Oliver Ditson Co., 1919.
> Useful as a basic text; is still regarded as a basic authority.

RUDOLF, MAX. *The Grammar of Conducting.* New York: G. Schirmer, Inc., 1950.
> Provides complete, authentic treatise on musicianly conducting.

SCHMID, ADOLF. *The Language of the Baton.* New York: G. Schirmer, Inc., 1937.
> Provides material useful for the conductor of the band, orchestra, or chorus.

VAN BODEGRAVEN, PAUL. *The School Music Conductor.* Chicago: Hall & McCreary Co., 1942.
> In addition to the usual diagrams and glossaries of musical terminology, this book suggests a philosophy of rehearsal as a guide to developing musicianship; is a good adjunct to some other text on conducting.

GENERAL EDUCATION AND
MUSIC EDUCATION

BRUBACHER, JOHN S. *Modern Philosophies of Education.* New York: McGraw-Hill Book Co., Inc., 1939.
> Studiously attempts to present and summarize viewpoints on the main educational philosophies; is important.

BRUBACHER, JOHN S., *et al. The Public Schools and Spiritual Values.* New York: Harper & Bros., 1944.
> Defends and surveys the non-material emphases, both as to content and objectives, in public education.

GEHRKENS, KARL W. *Introduction to School Music Teaching.* See listing under Chapter 4.

HOOD, MARGUERITE V., and SCHULTZ, E. J. *Learning Music Through Rhythm.* Boston: Ginn & Co., 1949.
> Provides helps for teachers of all grades; is equally useful for general teachers and specialist music teachers.

HORNE, HERMAN H. *This New Education.* New York: Abingdon Press, 1931.
> The author examines critically both pragmatic and behavioristic approaches to educational method; maintains that education, morality, and religion are closely related.

JOHNSTON, JOHN B. *Education for Democracy.* Minneapolis: University of Minnesota Press, 1934.
> Extends the content of an earlier book, *Liberal College in a Changing Society*; offers a philosophy and methodology for higher education in a democracy.

KANZELL, MAXWELL. *How to Read Music.* New York: Maxwell Kanzell, 1944.
> Discards movable *do* and number systems; presents an approach to music reading that is challenging and worthy of investigation.

MURSELL, JAMES L. *Principles of Musical Education.* New York: The Macmillan Co., 1927.
> A thoughtful, scholarly book, still important, based upon psychological findings.

NATIONAL SOCIETY FOR THE STUDY OF EDUCATION. Committee on Music Education, Guy Montrose Whipple (ed.). *Thirty-Fifth Yearbook.* Bloomington, Ind.: Public School Publishing Co., 1936.

PERHAM, BEATRICE. *Music in the New School.* See listing under Chapter 3.

WOEFEL, NORMAN. *Molders of the American Mind.* New York: Columbia University Press, 1933.
> Reviews critically what were in the author's time the modern philosophies of education in the United States; includes an examination of the social attitudes of seventeen leaders in education.

HISTORY OF MUSIC

ALLEN, WARREN DWIGHT. *Philosophies of Music History*. New York: American Book Co., 1939.
    Warns the student of history against overemphasizing Western civilization, conjecturing intemperately about origins, speaking too freely about development in music; surveys the important points of view of the different philosophies of history of music.

BURK, CASSIE, MEIERHOFFER, VIRGINIA, and PHILLIPS, CLAUDE A. *America's Musical Heritage*. Chicago: Laidlaw Bros., 1942.
    Presents the story of American music in a way that is suitable for junior high school children; adults will also enjoy this book.

DAVISON, ARCHIBALD, and APEL, WILLI. *Historical Anthology of Music*. Cambridge: Harvard University Press, Vol. I, 1946; Vol. II, 1950.
    Fills a vacancy that has long been a problem to teachers of music history; provides ample material for general study of medieval and Renaissance music.

DE JARNETTE, REVEN S. *Hollis Dann, His Life and Contribution to Music*. Boston: C. C. Birchard & Co., 1940.
    This account of an important leader in earlier music education provides an important orientation for the music education of today.

DICKINSON, EDWARD. *The Study of the History of Music*. New York: Charles Scribner's Sons, 1927.
    Provides a detailed, profound, and absolutely dependable account of the history of music; is authoritative, and is of special significance because the author was one of the pioneers in democratizing and developing processes of music appreciation.

EWEN, DAVID. *Composers of Yesterday*. New York: H. W. Wilson Co., 1937.
    Furnishes a biographical and critical guide to many of the most important composers of the past.

————. *Living Musicians*. New York: H. W. Wilson Co., 1940.
    This volume makes available information about musicians living up to 1940 that is not to be found easily elsewhere.

FERGUSON, DONALD NIVEN. *A History of Musical Thought*. New York: Appleton-Century-Crofts Co., Inc., 1948.
    Attempts to investigate the thinking out of which sprang the events in music's history; is a comprehensive study for a mature reader.

GRAF, MAX. *Modern Music*. New York: Philosophical Library, 1946.
    Portrays the changes in serious music from 1896; reminisces on Hindemith, Mahler, Schoenberg, and Stravinsky.

JOHNSON, H. EARLE. *Musical Interludes in Boston*. New York: Columbia University Press, 1943.
    Presents an attractive picture of music in the Boston of 1795–1830, accompanied by ample documentation from contemporary news releases and programs.

LÀNG, PAUL H. *Music in Western Civilization*. New York: W. W. Norton & Co., Inc., 1941.
This is a great book which is designed to show music's part in the making of Western civilization; it has been spoken of as a book, in its field, unrivaled in the English language.

McKINNEY, HOWARD D., and ANDERSON, W. R. *Music in History*. New York: American Book Co., 1940.
Studies anew music's place in artistic history; presents numerous illustrations and references to recordings.

MILLER, HUGH MILTON. *An Outline-History of Music*. New York: Barnes & Noble, Inc., 1947.
Furnishes comprehensive information in concise form; is valuable as an introductory reference book.

SACHS, CURT. *Rise of Music in the Ancient World*. New York: W. W. Norton & Co., Inc., 1943.
The author brings, as usual, a wealth of scholarship to a detailed study of a particular period in musical history.

SLONIMSKY, NICOLAS. *Music Since 1900*. New York: Coleman-Ross Co., 1949.
Combines palatably both history and criticism, and serves as a valuable reference work.

MATERIALS AND SOURCES OF MATERIALS FOR TEACHING MUSIC

Of great and important aid to the music educator is the service rendered by the Music Educators National Conference. Queries about physical equipment, architectural design, and teaching materials, books, music and literature are efficiently answered by the staff of the Conference; its office is located in Chicago. Many bulletins, pamphlets, and monographs are published by the Conference and made available at nominal charge to school authorities. Also, the United States Office of Education publishes bulletins covering a wide range of subjects pertaining to music education.

It would be beyond the purpose of this present volume to list the instrument manufacturing companies and the music and education publishing houses which efficiently and generously serve the music teaching profession. The several "series" of music methods, and the special collections of folk and art music, written, arranged, scored, and pedagogically presented, are readily obtainable.

There are several methods by which one may build up a good record collection. Many of the books on history of music suggest suitable recordings (Ferguson, Miller, McKinney and Anderson, and others). The several music series themselves suggest records.

The following record collections are important:

Elementary School

RCA Victor Record Library for Elementary Schools. 85 records. Grades 1–3; 4–6. Victor.

Secondary and Higher Schools

Anthologie Sonore. Gramophone Shop.
Columbia History of Music Series. Columbia.
Music of the Orient. Decca.
Two Thousand Years of Music. Decca.

Bibliographical Reference Sources

Book Review Digest. New York: H. W. Wilson Co.
Cumulative Book Index. New York: H. W. Wilson Co.
Education Index. New York: H. W. Wilson Co.
International Index of Periodicals. New York: H. W. Wilson Co.
Music Index. Detroit: Information Service, Inc.
Musical Literature List for Music School Libraries, National Association of Schools of Music. Published from time to time.
Readers Guide to Periodical Literature. New York: H. W. Wilson Co.
SHAW, CHARLES B. *List of Books for College Libraries.* Chicago: American Library Association, 1931. A supplement was published in 1940.
Standard Catalogue for Public Libraries. New York: H. W. Wilson Co., 1934. Supplements have been published from time to time.

Phonograph Record Selection

Encyclopedia of Records. New York: Gramophone Shop.
    Lists recordings from many catalogs both American and European; is not critically selective.

HALL, DAVID. *Records.* New York: Alfred A. Knopf, Inc., 1950.
    Makes critical recommendations about records released since 1947.

HAGGIN, BERNARD H. *Music on Records.* See listing under Appreciation of Music.

LEAVITT, HELEN S., and FREEMAN, WARREN S. *Recordings for the Elementary School.* New York: Ginn & Co., 1949.
    Provides source material for guiding the use of recordings in elementary music education.

MUSICIANSHIP

BAUMAN, ALVIN. *Elementary Musicianship.* New York: Prentice-Hall, Inc., 1947.
    Provides for student and teacher a book actually to be used and written in as a notebook; some have regarded the book as overly condescending to the novice.

CHAPPLE, STANLEY. *The Class Way to the Keyboard.* New York: Boosey-Hawkes-Belwin, 1934.
    Offers a musicianly approach to keyboard harmony; of limited usefulness in the United States because of the British musical terminology.

DOTY, EZRA W. *The Analysis of Form in Music.* New York: Appleton-Century-Crofts Co., Inc., 1947.

Serves as a workbook in the study of form and analysis; includes staff paper.

FIELDS, VICTOR A. *Training the Singing Voice.* New York: King's Crown Press, 1947.
Classifies and examines the mass of vocal teaching material; is of value especially to the new vocal teacher.

GEHRKENS, KARL W. *Music Notation and Terminology.* New York: Laidlaw Bros., 1930.
Furnishes complete and authoritative information about notation and terminology; the author is musical editor of *Webster's International Dictionary.*

GINGRICH, IRVING. *Contrapuntal Ear-Training.* Chicago: H. T. Fitzsimons Co., 1938.
Provides an important approach to developing the listening power by aurally studying contrapuntal examples.

HARDING, ROSAMOND E. M. *Origins of Musical Time and Expression.* New York: Oxford University Press, 1938.
Investigates history of the metronome; imitative tendencies in instrument building; story of pitch pipes; history of crescendo and decrescendo, forte and piano.

HINDEMITH, PAUL. *A Concentrated Course in Traditional Harmony.* New York: Associated Music Publishers, Inc., 1943.
An up-to-date presentation of traditional harmony; is best used under the guidance of a mature teacher.

NICOLL, IRENE HOWLAND, and DENNIS, CHARLES M. *Simplified Vocal Training.* New York: Carl Fischer, Inc., 1940.
Provides solid instruction and good materials for developing the singing voice; is in two parts: (1) principles, and (2) interpretation.

SHAW, W. WARREN, and LINDSAY, GEORGE L. *Educational Vocal Technique.* Vols. I and II. Philadelphia: Theodore Presser Co., 1936.
This complete treatment of problems confronting beginning voice students is adaptable in both class and private instruction.

SLONIMSKY, NICOLAS. *A Thing or Two About Music.* New York: Allen, Towne & Heath, Inc., 1948.
Amusing anecdotes dating from 1784, excerpted out of newspapers and magazines.

TOVEY, DONALD F. *Essays in Musical Analysis.* London: Oxford University Press, 1939.
These essays represent the work of many years in preparing program notes for the Reid Symphony Orchestra of Edinburgh.

VAN BODEGRAVEN, PAUL. *The School Music Conductor.* See listing under Conducting.

PERIODICALS

Educational Music Magazine. Chicago: Educational Music Bureau.
Étude. Bryn Mawr, Pa.: Theodore Presser Co.

Instrumentalist. Glen Ellyn, Ill.; Instrumentalist Co.
Music Educators Journal. Chicago: Music Educators National Conference.
Musical Quarterly. New York: G. Schirmer, Inc.
Musicology. Flushing, N. Y.: M and M Publications.
Notes. Washington, D.C.: Library of Congress.
School Musician. Chicago: School Musician Publishing Co.

PHYSICS OF MUSIC

BARTHOLOMEW, WILMER T. *Acoustics of Music.* New York: Prentice-Hall, Inc., 1942.
   Treats completely for the musician the physics of sound and music.

REFERENCE WORKS AND ENCYCLOPEDIAS

APEL, WILLI. *Harvard Dictionary of Music.* Cambridge: Harvard University Press, 1944.
   Provides excellent material for reference, especially in bibliography; suffers because it is a "one-man" book; is sometimes in error.
Grove's Dictionary of Music and Musicians. New York: The Macmillan Co., 1936–40.
   The third edition of 1928, with the supplementary volumes of later period, continues to be the indispensable reference work.
International Cyclopedia of Music and Musicians. See listing under Chapter 1.
Music Education Source Book. See listing under Chapter 4.
MUSIC EDUCATORS NATIONAL CONFERENCE YEARBOOKS. From 1919.
MUSIC TEACHERS NATIONAL ASSOCIATION. *Papers and Proceedings.* From 1906.
Oxford Companion to Music. New York: Oxford University Press, 1947.
   This dictionary of music, edited by Percy A. Scholes, serves as a useful manual and companion; it is not complete enough to be encyclopedic, but what it includes is dependably treated.

SINGING

FIELDS, VICTOR A. *Training the Singing Voice.* See listing under Musicianship.
KAGEN, SERGIUS. *On Studying Singing.* New York: Rinehart & Co., Inc., 1950.
   A timely, practical, authentic, and unromantic treatment of how to sing.
NICOLL, IRENE H., and DENNIS, CHARLES M. *Simplified Vocal Training.* See listing under Musicianship.

PIERCE, ANNE, and LIEBLING, ESTELLE. *Class Lessons in Singing*. See listing under Chapter 6.

SHAW, W. W., and LINDSAY, GEORGE L. *Educational Vocal Technique*. See listing under Musicianship.

VOCATIONAL OUTLETS FOR MUSIC

ABBOTT, GEORGE J. *Instrumental Music in the Public Schools*. See listing under Activities in Music.

ANDERSON, WILLIAM R. *Music as a Career*. New York: Oxford University Press, 1939.
  Provides authentic vocational information; is of British origin.

BARTON, FREDERICK B. *Music as a Hobby*. See listing under Appreciation of Music.

JOHNSON, HARRIET. *Your Career in Music*. See listing under Chapter 2.

TAUBMAN, H. H. *Music as a Profession*. New York: Charles Scribner's Sons, 1939.
  More than a vocational reference work, this book presents accurately and interestingly the salient facts about the profession of music.

INDEX OF NAMES

INDEX OF SUBJECTS